THE
ARAB MIND
CONSIDERED

Also by John Laffin

Fedayeen: The Arab-Israeli Dilemma
British Campaign Medals
Codes and Ciphers: Secret Writing Through the Ages
Anzacs at War
Women in Battle
Links of Leadership: Thirty Centuries of Command
Americans in Battle
The Hunger to Come: The Food and Population Crises
New Geography: 1968–1969
New Geography: 1970–1971
Anatomy of Captivity
and other titles

THE
ARAB MIND
CONSIDERED

A Need for Understanding

by JOHN LAFFIN

Taplinger Publishing Company : New York

First published in the United States in 1975 by
TAPLINGER PUBLISHING CO., INC.
New York, New York

ransmitted
nechanical,
rmation storage
rented, without
cept by a reviewer
ction with a review
ner, or broadcast.

The Arab Mind.

Library of Congress Catalog Card Number: 75-5042

ISBN 0-8008-0294-2

Contents

have spoken at length with thousands of people from nearly every Arab country. The most famous was President Nasser, whom I interviewed in Cairo in 1956. The most infamous were young Arab assassins in a terrorist training camp in 'Fatahland', Lebanon. I was once nursed, when ill, by a nomadic Bedouin family and I have close, and, I hope, enduring relationships with several educated Arab families. 'Word of an Englishman', I have told the truth about their society.

I owe much to my wife in the preparation of this book. She accompanies me on most of my journeys, helps me with research and types my manuscripts.

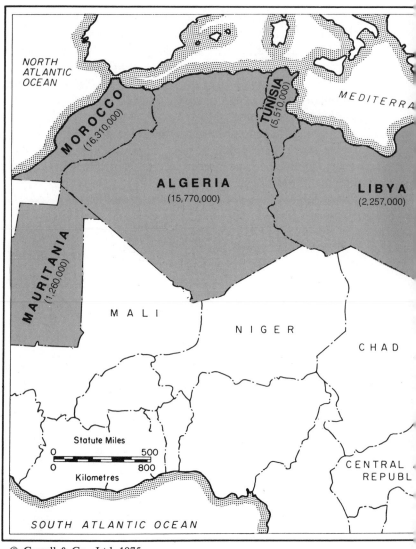

NORTH
ATLANTIC
OCEAN

MEDITERRA

MOROCCO
(16,310,000)

TUNISIA
(5,510,000)

ALGERIA
(15,770,000)

LIBYA
(2,257,000)

MAURITANIA
(1,260,000)

M A L I

N I G E R

CHAD

CENTRAL
REPUBL

Statute Miles

0 ⊢⊣⊢⊣ 500

0 ⊢⊣⊢⊣ 800

Kilometres

SOUTH ATLANTIC OCEAN

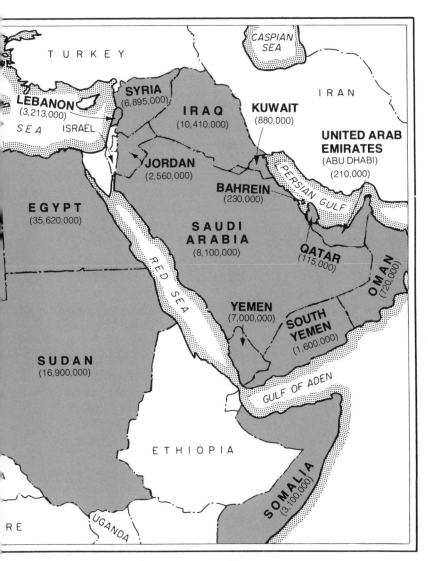

THE ARAB WORLD

The twenty Arab states are shown with their approximate populations (as of 1973).

THE
ARAB MIND
CONSIDERED

1 *The Torments of History*

'Whoever loves the Prophet, loves the Arabs . . . whomever God has guided to Islam knows that Mohammad is the chosen of the prophets, and the Arabs the chosen of the nations, and Arabic, the chosen of the languages.' al-Tha'alibi, eleventh-century writer.

'Western civilization and its heritage, for which Europe and America fear so much, live only on the debris of the East and would not flourish if they had not sucked its blood. That is the astonishing truth.' Anwar Sadat, later President of Egypt, *Story of Arab Unity*, Cairo, 1957.

Centuries ago, history 'turned wrong' for the Arabs, an Egyptian historian told me in 1973. This change in direction with its consequent trauma was brought about by enemies jealous of their religion and progress, many Arabs believe, and this conviction is a principal reason for the great psychological sickness which fell like a plague upon the Arab race.

Yet they are correct, history *did* 'turn wrong', if we interpret this to mean that it did not proceed in the way that the Arabs had every reason to expect it to go. In the seventh century the prophet Mohammad promised them glory and dominion and for centuries they found it. Mohammad gave the Arabs a new Islamic community permeated by a great sense of pride and purpose. His successors scored the name 'Arab' across the three continents of Asia, Africa and Europe and if the means were often bloody they were no more so than those practised before and since by other empire-builders.

The Arabic-speaking people of Arabia founded, developed and exploited a vast empire stretching from Central Asia across the Middle East and North Africa to the Atlantic. Almost

15

everywhere they were a ruling minority, invincible, it seemed, under the inspiration of their national religion and their consciousness of being Allah's chosen people.

Great military victories brought under Arab rule, among others, the Persians, Syrians, Egyptians, increasing numbers of whom were converted to the Islamic faith and to the Arabic language. Arabic civilization grew rich and diverse and the Arab sense of heritage and tradition became as perceptual as it had earlier been merely conceptual. In many areas the conquerors did not interfere with the internal civil and religious administration of the conquered peoples. This enlightened control was particularly welcome to those who had been the subjects of much harsher Byzantine masters. Even the Christian population of Egypt and Syria, while detesting Islam, preferred its rule to that of the Byzantines.

Despite civil wars and inter-Islam strife, the Empire grew. In Central Asia the Arabs took Herat, Kabul and Bokhara; in North Africa they pressed steadily towards Tunisia and kept their eyes on the Atlantic. They built a Mediterranean fleet and, in A.D. 655, won the first great naval victory over the Byzantines.

As military strength grew so economy developed, and in the eighth century it was sophisticated, prosperous and vast. In this relatively peaceful period, from Persian Gulf ports, from Aden and the Red Sea, Moslem merchants were constantly on the move with a driving spirit of enterprise perhaps equalled only by the Japanese in the mid-twentieth century. They travelled by sea to India, Ceylon, the East Indies and China, trading in silks, spices, aromatics, wood, tin, paper, saddlery, peacocks, drugs, elephants, tigers and doorlocks, and much else. Other Arab traders used overland routes to India and China, opening up and influencing much of Central Asia. These businessmen saw profit in people as much as in material things, so they traded in slave girls, hydraulic engineers (from China), marble-workers and eunuchs. In Africa, Arabs were travelling far and dangerously, mainly in search of gold and slaves.

Their trade, though not through Arabs personally, reached as far as Sweden and the Baltic lands. The earliest known Swedish coinage is based on the Arabic dirham weight and old Icelandic literature contains several Arabic words. Because of inplacable hostility from Christendom, Arabs had not yet reached Western Europe but Jews acted as middlemen between them and Europeans. Commercialism was so complex by the tenth century that the Arab world had banks, government and private, though both types had to be staffed by Jews and Christians because of the Islam ban on usury.

Despite civil wars and rebellions in their own State, some of them serious, the Arabs pushed further afield and any reverses seemed only to make them more determined. They occupied Palermo, Sicily, in 831, and used it as a base for expansion. With garrisons at Bari and Taranto, they threatened Naples and Rome and northern Italy, and for two years compelled a Pope to pay tribute—a measure of their power.

History was certainly going 'right' for the Arabs of the time, who were not mere bandits eager only to sack their new territories. Sicily is a good example of their principles of occupation. Experts in irrigation, they extended cultivation and imported from Arabia oranges, mulberries, sugar-cane, date-palms and cotton. It was a remarkable administration.

Arabs had first reached Spain in 710 and within a mere eight years they had occupied the greater part of the peninsula. Their administration in Spain has been much libelled by Spanish historians; the truth is that it was tolerant, liberal and almost socialistic. For instance, the domination of the nobles and the clergy was removed and, by sweeping land reforms, land was distributed to a large new class of peasant farmers who quickly made Moslem Spain agriculturally prosperous. Further Arab colonists, mostly from Syria, settled along the Mediterranean coastlands.

The ready acceptance of Moslem overlordship is clearly shown by the vast numbers of conversions to Islam among the native-born Spaniards. The Archbishop of Seville in the mid-ninth century had the Bible translated into Arabic for his own congregation. Other bishops travelled on diplomatic missions for the Moslem rulers. All this indicated lessening dissension and by the tenth century the Arabs, Berbers and Spanish Moslems were unified culturally and politically.

An Arab army had crossed the Pyrenees into France but their advance was checked by Charles Martel at Poitiers in 732 and they retreated to Spain. They made no further move across the mountains. Christianity was gaining military strength in northern Spain and gradually the Moslems were overpowered in a centuries' long trial of strength. By the end of the thirteenth century they held only the province and city of Granada, which they lost in a great battle fought against the armies of Castile and Aragon on January 2, 1492. The Arabs were driven from Spain.

It has been Spanish custom to revile the Arabs but they enriched Iberian life immeasurably, giving it a cultural richness, an economic prosperity and a political security rare in its history.

All Western Europe benefited from Arab culture in Spain. Many Christian scholars came to study under Arabic-speaking Moslem and Jewish teachers. Great Greek teachings reached the West through Arabic translations found in Spain, and science and philosophy profited from Arab infusions. The Arabs had produced nothing less than a new civilization with an amalgam of many peoples of different faiths and cultures. For the first time in history the Arabs had united territories stretching from the borders of China to those of Italy and France. But even more significantly the Arabs had united in a single society the formerly conflicting cultures of the Mediterranean, the Near East and the Middle East.

As will be seen in later chapters, the inner Islamic world was in a state of decay by the eleventh century but the year 1492 in distant Spain marks the irrevocable point at which history 'turned wrong'. The Arab–Islam world was no longer advancing and was no longer progressive. The Arabs seemed to have lost their position as Mohammad's 'chosen of the nations'. The decay was never checked and the former conquerors became subject peoples ruled by many races of foreigners. No Arab was strong enough to arrest the decline.

Yet consider Arabic achievements centuries ago. When Western Europe was abysmally stagnant under the dead weight of the Dark Ages, Arabic literature, philosophy, mathematics and medicine were flourishing. A reverence for learning and intellectual experiment characterized society in many, though not all, regions. In the twentieth century experiment was non-existent and no Arab was contributing anything of value to the liberal arts, the humanities or the sciences.

The earlier Arabs had been a proud and noble people, less prone to excesses than their contemporaries of other races and generally better educated in their time than those of Western Europe. Collectively, they had skills and abilities matched only by the Greeks and Romans. Probably, the names of more brilliant Arab individuals have come down to us than from any race other than the Greeks and Romans. In the early decades of the twentieth century, the Arab world was decadent and ignorant and without nobility. No wonder an historian could complain that history had 'turned wrong'.

What, other than history, could be blamed for the obvious fact that in the earlier part of the twentieth century, Western peoples regarded the Arabs as nothing more than romantic figures who wore colourful clothing, rode camels, plotted in casbahs, lusted in harems, lived in oases and had been dashingly led by Lawrence of Arabia in World War I? That this was a travesty and a stereotyped generalization only emphasizes the degree of Arab decay.

After the establishment of the State of Israel in 1948 the stereotype of an Arab was as an enemy of the Jews, but he was still a remote and ill-defined figure. While some Englishmen and Frenchmen had a clearer picture because of more than a century's close association with Arabs, images were still rigid because relationships were rigid. The British and French were rulers and administrators, the Arabs a people who seemed to have lost all confidence. They were capable, the Westerners said, of all kinds of dirty tricks. In our time film-makers have exploited the Arab mercilessly with *The Desert Song* and Marlene Dietrich's *Morocco* at either end of a wildly oscillating value scale. In a hundred films set anywhere from Tangier to Baghdad villainous Arabs dealt in arms, secrets, drugs and women—and knifed anyone who got in the way.

If the Arabs had attitudes and politics they did not begin to touch the euphoric, complacent mainstream of Western life until the commission of terrorist acts by Palestinian Arabs —such as hijacking and destruction of aircraft, the murder of hostages and the massacre of Israeli athletes at Munich in 1972. Arabs as a whole were then labelled as unstable and murderous, but they remained a distant threat. The public is not involved because a letter bomb kills only one man, terrorists kill only small groups—diplomats in Khartoum, for instance—a bloody attempted coup in Morocco is as bloodily quelled, but Arabs are the only victims. The Western world is uninvolved. An Arab assassinated Robert Kennedy but left the other 210 million Americans untouched. Then came the great disclosure of Arab power: by declaring, late in 1973, an Oil War on the West and on Japan, the Arabs entered the life of every person in the developed world.

Ostensibly, the Oil War was a lever to force Israel to release land which the Arabs feel belongs to them—Sinai, the Golan Heights, the West Bank of the Jordan, Jerusalem—and to return Palestine to Arab rule. The Arabs said to the West, in effect, 'Stop supporting Israel and induce her to return Arab land or we will cut off your oil supplies.' But this was a secondary threat. In fact, the first declaration of the Oil War of 1973 was a sharp increase in prices before the Arab–Israeli shooting war and it has little connection with Arab animosity to Jews. Arab politicians have kept the 'Palestinian issue' alive to use it as an excuse whenever needed. They are bored with the Palestinians, but for as long as they can be exploited for political capital they have their uses. This applies to Israel, in itself no threat to the Arab world. But the responsibility for internal problems can often be avoided by blaming them on an external 'enemy'. In this case, too, the Israeli enemy is demonstrably prosperous in a previously barren land. This is enough to establish a grievance in minds receptive to propaganda.

History will see the Oil War as an attempt to make history 'turn right'. It became one of the principal duties of the Caliphs —the successors of Mohammad—to extend the faith and Moslem-ruled territory. Islamic law does not recognize the possibility of peace with the 'unbelievers and infidels' although expediency might require discretion rather than valour and long periods of truce. That part of the world which is not Islamic is known in Islamic theology as 'the territory of war'. As the more militant Arabs see it, Mohammad's task will not be fulfilled as long as non-Moslems remain in control of any part of the globe.

Arab leaders quickly learnt in 1973, from the far-ranging reconnaissance of Saudi Arabia's Sheikh Yamani, that the European nations, and others, had no stomach for a fight. As hooked on oil as any alcoholic on liquor, the 'developed' world was ready to grovel for its next shot—and to pay any price for it. The unconquerable West—the 'predators, imperialists and colonialists, the unbelievers'—were being brought to their knees, by economic means, for the first time in many centuries. This gave profound satisfaction to Arabs from the Arabian Gulf to the Atlantic, for it wiped away some of the shame of centuries of 'humiliation'. History was now pointing in the right direction.

This book, then, is an attempt to show how the Arab personality and mind has developed; to explain how a vigorous, intelligent race became leaderless, confused and apathetic. It is an attempt to define and describe Arab attitudes, which are assuredly different from those of other people. At the same time, I must emphasize that the characteristics discussed here are not *peculiar* to the Arabs. Exaggeration, conceit, pride and vacillation—to mention a few traits—are commonplace among other

races. The difference between Arabs and most others is one of
intensity of certain emotions and behavioural patterns, such as
shame and violence. I refer to particular Arab weaknesses. Men
and women of other nationalities have their own weaknesses,
but this book is not about *them*. I am dealing with a history of
remarkable length, so some authorial generalizations are
inevitable; of all countries in the world the longest recorded
history is connected with an area that is occupied by Arabs;
chronologically it covers 7,000 or more years of settled human
life, two-thirds of which are well documented by written
records. The Arab world covers 5,300,000 square miles, consists
of 20 states* and at least 139 million people and they range in
temperament from the nomadic Bedouin to the urbanized
dwellers of Beirut and Tunis. Their leaders range from the
passionate fanatic to the rational pragmatist. Where specific
exceptions might invalidate a generalization, I have stated them.

Dr Sania Hamady, herself an Arab and one of the greatest
authorities on Arab psychology, says that to the individual
'life is a fearful test' for 'modern Arab society is ruthless, stern
and pitiless . . . worships strength and has no compassion for
weakness'. Hamady says that Arab social life is 'full of pain,
bitterness and insecurity'.

For the sake of rational relationships, Westerners must understand the Arab. On the personal level, for instance, the Arab,
accustomed to signs of emotivity and impulsiveness in his
speech, tries to communicate a certain idea to Westerners in
ways they cannot comprehend. He shouts, he gets excited, he
boasts, he threatens, he rebukes. To the Westerner the atmosphere seems tense, even dangerous. But this is the normal way
in which Arabs communicate with each other. Conversely the
Arab will interpret Western calmness as lack of responsiveness
and sympathy to his ideas. Trying to impress on an audience
the fact that he means what he says, the Arab resorts to emphatic

* They are: Algeria, Bahrein, Egypt, Iraq, Jordan, Kuwait, Lebanon, Libya,
Mauritania, Morocco, Oman, Qatar, Saudi Arabia, Somalia, Sudan, Syria,
Tunisia, United Arab Emirates, Yemen Arab Republic, People's Democratic
Republic of Yemen (South Yemen).

assertion and exaggeration. If he does not emphasize his point he is afraid that the listener may think he means the opposite.

On the political level, civil strife is a permanent condition in Arab countries and the natural function of a government is to be oppressive. Unless a Westerner can grasp this basic fact it is difficult for him to understand the Arab way of life.

In international affairs both Hamady and E. A. Westermarck,* another distinguished orientalist, have noted that the Arabs possess 'one striking characteristic'. Their reaction to failures and slurs is often offensive rather than defensive. As Westermarck says, 'This inclination seems to have been partly institutionalized and greatly affected by the traditional call for jihad.' Jihad is holy war.

Hamady says of her own people: 'Arabs' laziness, lack of perseverance and irresponsibility, their lack of team spirit, co-operation and punctuality, their procrastination, and lying must be understood to know what to expect of them and how to approach them. . . . To the Arab, provided no one knows, any wrong is permissible. Secrecy licenses every kind of behaviour and frees the individual from any pangs of conscience. . . . The Arab is human but not humane. . . .'

Even the casual observer of groups in city streets and villages will notice extremes of friendship and enmity expressed in words and gestures; disputes break out frequently and suddenly, with a strong tendency to physical violence and loud argument, and then end as suddenly. Friendships become profound, with the exchange of complete confidence and allowance of little personal privacy, and then, out of jealousy or misunderstanding, quickly turn to absolute hatred and enmity.

We must understand more about Arab violence and its causes. In Arab countries between 1948 and 1973—a mere quarter of a century—no fewer than eighty revolts occurred, most of them bloodily violent. Thirty of these revolts were successful and twenty-two major political leaders were murdered.

* E. A. Westermarck, *Pagan Survivals in Mohammedan Civilization*, Macmillan, London, 1933.

Until their oil runs out the Arabs can be 'violent' in other ways. They can dictate the West's economy and life-style and even after that their hostility towards Israel—which is a symbol of the West—will feed their Islamic fervour and their earlier historical ambition of world domination. Only by understanding the Arab can we help him to expel those devils which drive him—the terrifying torments of his religion, his sexual frustrations and obsessions, his paralysing sense of shame. All these make Arab society one of great strain and tension. We can ease that tension, or at least prevent it from being strung even tighter, by realizing that facts cannot be presented nakedly to the Arab; they need to be masked so as to avoid any offence or injury to the Arab's inner self. It is almost impossible for the Arab to be objective about himself or to accept calmly someone else's criticism of him. It is difficult for him to live in peace with himself and with others.

The sources for my own understanding of the Arabs are varied. Over a period of twenty years I have visited most Arab countries and I know many Arabs as friends. I have shared frugal meals with Bedouin and have never told them of my inability to digest their food, taken part in interminable conversations and heard the most outrageous lies (for the Arab there are various kinds of truth, as will be seen later), and I have learnt from experience that sooner or later all Arab hospitality must be paid for in favours, introductions, gifts or reciprocal hospitality. And I have witnessed both major facets of the dichotomous Arab personality—great generosity and savage cruelty.

My more academic sources are largely Arabic—scholars, political and military leaders, journalists, poets. I have either read their work or have spoken to them, usually at great length. Similarly, I have studied the work of leading Western 'Arabists' and orientalists or have interviewed them. Nobody knows as much about the Arabs as the Israeli scholars from the universities of Jerusalem, Tel Aviv, Haifa, many hundreds of whom have spent vast amounts of time studying in depth every facet of Arab history—its politics, literature, religion and psychology. They have the special incentive of survival to be accurate in their findings; mistakes in reading Arab intentions —such as those which occurred before the October 1973 war— can be dangerous.

Having read much that Israeli scholars have written, I can say that their information is much the same as that from Arab and Western observers. Since scholars of various nationalities tend to begin from a different premise this uniformity at the conclusion is interesting. Unfortunately, anybody who writes about the Arabs and is critical, no matter how constructively, runs the risk of being told by Arabs that he is pro-Israeli and therefore anti-Arab. This applies even to Arabs who offer criticisms. This conclusion-jumping is another important facet of the Arab mind.

My concern is for the truth and I can illustrate the truth as well as tell it. On April 25, 1967, a momentous event occurred in Damascus. The Syrian Army magazine, *Jaysh al'Sha'b* (The People's Army) published an article by an unknown second lieutenant, Ibrahim Khalas, entitled 'The Means of Creating a New Arab Man'.

Discussing the development of Arab society and evolution of Arab civilization, Lieutenant Khalas urged the creation of a new Arab socialist, a man 'who believes that Allah, religions, feudalism, capital and all the values which prevailed in the pre-existing society were no more than stuffed puppets in the museums of history. . . . There is only one value—absolute faith in the new man of destiny who relies only on himself and on his own contribution to humanity. . . . He knows that his inescapable end is death and nothing beyond death . . . no heaven and no hell. . . . We have no need of men who kneel and beg for grace and pity. . . .'

Lieutenant Khalas was not reacting against 'Israeli irritations' —the Six-Day War was two months ahead. At the time Syria was in the grip of an apathy induced by suppression of free speech, the confiscation of property and control of movement, among many other restrictions. But the magazine article, expressing sentiments never before published in a revolutionary Arab state, stung the public to a fury. Here was an attack on Allah and religion in an official journal. With tension increasing dangerously, on May 5 the Government arrested Lieutenant Khalas and the editor of *Jaysh al'Sha'b*. Next day, in a further conciliatory move the Government-sponsored *Al-Thaura* (The Revolution) proclaimed its respect for religion and then came a Government announcement that the offending article had been planted by the C.I.A., other evil Americans, the British, the Jordanians, the Saudis and the Zionists.

When this did not placate the public, the editor and author were tried and on May 11 both were sentenced to life imprisonment with hard labour. Only a complete change of government will give them a chance of freedom.

This incident is profoundly significant for it shows the still great power of Islam, the disinclination of an Arab society to accept new ideas and criticism, and the lengths to which Arab authority will go in punishing deviance from traditional belief. Lieutenant Khalas was a Syrian patriot and a proud Arab seeking to find a new identity in the turbulent twentieth century. His plight is that of the whole Arab nation, a nation doing violence to itself and to others in its efforts to reshape history.

2 *Mohammad and the Koran*

'Arabs could be swung on an idea as on a cord, for the unpledged allegiance of their minds made them obedient servants.' T. E. Lawrence, *The Seven Pillars of Wisdom*.

'Without the Koran the Arabs would have neither the arts and humanities nor law.' Ali Husni al-Kharbutli, Professor of Islamic Studies, University of Ain Shams, Cairo.

Arabs are concerned with the definition of an Arab in a way that would never occur to people of other races to define themselves. It is almost as if by evolving a definition they gain confidence from it. Also, any definition invites exclusions, an appeal to the chauvinistic mind. Intellectuals and theologians differ on the terms. The simplest is that an Arab is anybody who speaks Arabic as his mother tongue.

The Lebanese scholar, Clovis Maqsud, has written: 'An Arab is one whose "destiny" is, either by force of circumstances or intentionally, bound to the Arab world as a whole. . . . Whoever is descended from Kurdish, Negro, or Armenian stock but has inhabited an Arab country, becomes an Arab by force of circumstances and by reason of the free association of his own destiny with that of the Arab world.'

Many Arabs would agree with Professor Gibb of Harvard that: 'All those are Arabs for whom the central fact of history is the mission of Mohammad and the memory of the Arab empire and who in addition cherish the Arabic tongue and its cultural heritage as their common possession.'

While Mohammad's mission is paramount, the pre-Islamic history of the Arabs cannot be ignored for it established traditions, customs and thought-processes which are still important in Arab life.

The pre-Mohammad history of the Bedouin particularly is mainly a record of wars, or rather of guerrilla conflicts, in which a great deal of raiding and plundering was accomplished, as a rule without serious bloodshed. There was no lack of shouting; volleys of taunts were exchanged; camels and women were carried off. Many skirmishes but few pitched battles took place in an Homeric kind of warfare that demanded much individual exertion and gave ample opportunity for single-handed heroics. To write a true history of such Bedouin feuds is impossible; all stories that have come down to us are crystallized round poems and all too often the narratives have been invented.

Above all, blood called for blood. This obligation obsessed the conscience of the pagan Arabs. Vengeance, with them, was 'almost a physical necessity, which if it be not obeyed will deprive its subject of sleep, of appetite, of health'.* It was a tormenting thirst which nothing would quench except blood, a disease of honour tantamount to a madness, although it rarely prevented the sufferer from approaching his task with coolness and circumspection. Vengeance was taken upon the murderer, if possible, or else upon one of his fellow-tribesmen. Usually this ended the matter, but in some cases it was the beginning of a blood-feud in which the entire kin of both parties were involved; for example, the murder of Kulayd led to the Forty Years' War between the Bakr and Taghlib tribes. The slain man's next of kin might accept an indemnity commonly paid in camels—the coin of the country—as atonement for him, though this was in no sense a compromise.

The Bedouin view of life was hedonistic. Love, wine, gambling, hunting, the pleasures of song and romance, the brief, pointed, and elegant expression of wit and wisdom—these things he knew to be good. Even battle was 'good'. Beyond all this the Bedouin saw only the grave, as the poet Hamasa wrote:

* R. A. Nicholson, *Literary History of the Arabs*, 1907.

'Roast meat and wine: the swinging ride
On a camel sure and tried,
Which her master speeds amain
O'er low dale and level plain:
Women marble-white and fair
Trailing gold-fringed raiment rare:
Opulence, luxurious ease,
With the lute's soft melodies—
Such delights hath our brief span;
Time is Change, Time's fool is Man,
Wealth or want, great store or small,
All is one since Death's are all.'

The Arab nomads before Mohammad had a religion of kinds, a form of polydaemonism related to the paganism of the ancient Semites. It included some gods in the true sense who were recognized far beyond the boundaries of tribal cults. The three most important were Manat, Uzza and Allat, all subject to an even higher deity, usually called Allah. There was no priesthood and the nomads carried their gods in a red tent, always prominent in battle. Gradually some nomads became settled, as at Mecca, where clans might have a communal shrine with some kind of symbol. In Mecca they had a cube-shaped building known as the Ka'ba which became the Islamic holy of holies. Other peoples lived in Arabia apart from the many different nomadic Arab tribes—Jews and Judaized Arabs were everywhere and Christian settlements were firmly established. The population of Mecca was diverse and into it, some time between the years A.D. 570 and 580, was born Mohammad. Brought up as a poor orphan, probably by his grandfather, Mohammad acquired wealth and position by marrying Khadija, the widow of a rich merchant several years older than himself. According to Moslem tradition he was illiterate. He first heard the Call in his thirty-ninth year—a call to bring an Arabic revelation to the Arabs, such as other races had already received in their own languages.

He began to preach in Mecca but made little progress, so in

the year 622 he moved to Medina, 280 miles away. This migration—or Hijra in Arabic—is the starting point of the Moslem calendar. Under the policy which Mohammad evolved, political and religious objectives were not distinct and never after became distinct. He led raids on merchant caravans—a natural and legitimate occupation to the Arabs—and increased his power, wealth and prestige. In March 624, with 300 Moslems, he surprised a Meccan caravan at Badr. The raiders' achievements and booty in this 'battle' are celebrated in the Koran as an expression of divine goodwill.

Mohammad's new religion was Islam and the word is significant. Used to indicate the whole religion and the civilization built on its foundation, it is derived from a verb *aslama*, which means to surrender or to be whole, unbroken, and by extension to be safe and sound. Literally, the verb form of *islam*—a word derived from *aslama*—means to deliver over in a sound condition; and *islam* itself means the act of giving oneself to Allah. In this way the common definition of Islam, submission, is derived. The term Moslem denotes one who has 'surrendered'. Another word used almost synonymously with *islam* is *iman*, meaning an act of belief, faith, or trust. Scholars emphasize the difference in spirit between these two words. Islam is an act of submission of oneself which seems to have been distinguished from belief or trust: an overt yielding to the religious system by doing certain things required by it, as distinct from belief or trust in God as a matter of conviction. The distinction between these two ideas appears in the Koran (sura xlix, 14) where it is clearly implied that Mohammad's followers were to regard themselves as merely *professing* Islam until faith 'found its way into your hearts', whereupon they could call themselves *believers*. Even today there are two words to denote the members of the Islamic community: *mu'min*, one who trusts in Allah, and *moslem*, one who has submitted himself to Allah.

Islam is not based on freely given obedience to great principles of action. The rules that govern the life of the Moslem are a system of minute legalism controlling every action. This system has the fascination of an absolute authority that lays down simple rules and calls for confident obedience. A stirring appeal to *l'homme moyen sensuel*, the normal virile man who desires satisfaction for his senses and the discipline of a simple rule of life, is made by the simple creed that is a combined faith, a bond of union and a battle-cry. It is a creed of a oneness and greatness of Allah and of His prophet Mohammad, exercised through the eternal authority of unalterable rule laid down in the Koran;* by the daily drill of the uniform prayer-motions; by the magic of the chanted rhythm of words; by the clear proud minaret call of the muezzin—'Come to prayer; prayer is better than sleep'. It is demonstrated, too, by the self-discipline of the annual celebration of Ramadan—thirty days of fasting during the daylight hours—and by the decisive law of the scimitar for the infidel, loot for the victorious warrior, and a Paradise of maidens and feasting for the heroic dead.

The law is civil and religious. It is the law of the State, enforced by the State, but its whole sanction is in the suras (chapters) of Mohammad which came verbally through him from Allah. This oneness of religion and state-law means that conversion from Islam to another faith is treachery to the State and is logically punishable by death.

The whole system is based on the traditions and the practice of Mohammad, 'Allah is great; Allah is one; and Mohammad is His prophet.' Mohammad washed, spoke, dressed in such a way; gave such and such divinely revealed orders. These suras are embodied in the Koran, which to the Moslem is the absolute, verbally unalterable, eternal Word of Allah. Civilization, therefore, is stereotyped, standardized, cast in a mould, and Islam is logically incapable of reform. As Lord Cromer said, 'Reformed Islam is Islam no longer.'

Under the impact of Mohammad's preaching of the new religion, the Jews and later the Christians were accused of having falsified their own scriptures in order to conceal the

---

* Koran (*Qu'ran*) is derived from the Arabic root *qara'a* 'to read', and means reading aloud or chanting.

prophecies of Mohammad's advent. As punishment, Mohammad had some Jewish tribes exterminated.

For the Moslem, Mohammad was the last and greatest of the apostles of Allah, sent as the Seal of the Prophecy to bring the final revelation of God's word to Mankind.

He did this in the 114 suras of the Koran which, whatever its moral and literary merits, is the greatest burden the Arabs have ever been given to bear. The Koran consists of the revelations or commands which Mohammad professed to have received from time to time through the angel Gabriel as a message direct from Allah; and which, under a supposed Divine direction, he delivered to those about him. At the time of the inspiration, or shortly after, Mohammad recited each passage to the 'Companions' or followers, and someone among them would write it on palm leaves, leather, stones or whatever was to hand. These divine messages continued for twenty-three years.

Because the Koran was revealed in Arabic it struck away support for all other dialects and provided the Arabs with one language, the language of the Koran. This important foundation of the nation was fixed and the new movement guaranteed the perpetuation of linguistic unity. Arabic became the greatest common denominator and those who spoke it had proof of belonging to the Arab race. The Arabs had vague notions about a common stock and descent, and this feeling of a unified origin crystallized in the distinction between Bedouin Arabs, genuine Arabs, and naturalized Arabs. But the new movement did not encourage the perpetuation of vague lineage to all ancestors. It emphasized the language, considering it as a total framework within which people might truly belong. Arabs of all peoples were regarded as those whose language most closely resembled that of the Koran. Coming out into the world—that is, out of the Arabian Peninsula—the Arabs carried this distinction with them.

An understanding of Arab motivations is impossible without an understanding of the impact of the Koran upon them. They see it as a miracle. According to Ali Husni al-Kharbutli,

Professor in Islamic Studies at the University of Ain Shams, Cairo, Mohammad himself said that it was impossible to contrive or reproduce anything like the Koran 'and that is why the believers turn to him faithfully'. The same writer, noting that the Koran is written neither in verse nor in free prose nor in measured, rhyming lines, calls it a 'composition that pleases, whose words have an agreeable ring and express lofty thoughts'.

One of the most agreeable and lofty thoughts appears in sura iii, 'The Imrans': 'You are the noblest nation that has ever been raised up for mankind. You enjoin justice and forbid evil. You believe in Allah.'

The many Arab Koranic scholars say that all literary figures of speech and all styles of rhetoric are found in the book. This is not so, but certainly the Arabs found in the language of the Koran great beauty and style; it was an object of admiration and wonder. They began to imitate it, to such an extent that some writers abandoned poetry, as was the case with Labid ibn Rabi'a, one of the authors of the *Mu'allaqat*, poems traditionally written just before the Koran. Each time he was asked to recite one of the poems he would reply, 'God has given me something better instead,' and he would recite a sura from the Koran.

The major drift of Islamic thought has been to resist the new. This tendency went so far that, in the judgment of the British orientalist D. S. Margoliuth, for a long time the Moslem Arabs remained intellectually silent under the weight of the Koran. This book, by its own account (sura xii, 111) an explanation of everything, was sent down on a night when all things were made clear (sura xliv, 3) and overlooks nothing (sura vi, 38). Hence, it seemed to make all other writing superfluous or dangerous.

In 'The Imrans' appears an injunction not to question the tenets of the Koran. 'There is no god but Him, the Mighty, the Wise One. It is He who has revealed to you the Koran. Some of its verses are precise in meaning . . . and others are ambiguous. Those whose hearts are infected with disbelief follow the ambiguous part, so as to create dissension by seeking to explain it. But no one knows its meaning except Allah.'

33

The Arab Mind Considered

Similarly, the Koran forbids experiment. 'Do not follow what you do not know.'

Much of the Koran translated into English or other languages loses its power but, as a multilingual Arab has told me, in Arabic it 'takes a man out of the world and gives him peace'. Some critics see the Koran as one of the great literary master-pieces but many European readers view it as obscure, tiresome and uninteresting—'a farrago of long-winded narratives and prosaic exhortations, quite unworthy to be named in the same breath with the prophetical books of the Old Testament', according to R. A. Nicholson, authority on Arabic literature. Nicholson says, 'One may peruse the greater part of the volume, beginning with the first chapter, and find but a few passages of genuine enthusiasm to relieve the prevailing dullness. It is in short suras placed at the end of the Koran that we must look for evidence of Mohammad's prophetic gift. These are the earliest of all; in these the flame of inspiration burns purely and its natural force is not abated.'

That the Koran is open to many translations and interpretations is clear from comparisons of the various English-language versions.

Mohammad is the Messenger of God, and those who are with him are hard against the unbelievers, merciful one to another. Thou seest them bowing, prostrating, seeking bounty from God and good pleasure. Arthur J. Arberry, *The Koran Translated*.

Mohammad is God's apostle. Those who follow him are ruthless to the unbelievers but merciful to one another. You see them adoring on their knees, seeking the grace of Allah and His good will. N. J. Dawood, *The Koran* (translated).

A great difference exists between 'ruthless' and 'hard against'; and between 'adoring and seeking grace' compared with 'bowing, prostrating, seeking bounty and good pleasure'.

Similarly, throughout his translation Arberry refers to 'God' while Dawood as consistently refers to 'Allah'. The use of 'God' is misleading, as the word and what it stands for is Western. By the logic Arberry appears to use it would be as valid among Christians to refer to their deity as 'Allah'.

The sound of the Arabic language of the Koran certainly influences Arabs (and Moslems generally) in a profound way but they are even more influenced by *what* the Koran says. In the briefest of terms—to be amplified by quotation—it promises delight to believers and damnation to unbelievers; it is both a licence and a limitation; it is defiantly dogmatic but it has escape clauses—'You shall not kill *without good cause*'; 'Do not interfere with the property of orphans *without the best of motives*'; 'Allah has forbidden you the flesh of beasts that die a natural death, blood, and pig's meat; also any flesh consecrated in the name of any but Allah. *But whoever is constrained to eat of it without intending to be a rebel or transgressor*, will find Allah merciful and forgiving.'*

Mohammad quite blatantly used the Koran to get himself out of at least one predicament, and perhaps in doing so showed himself as more of a mortal man than many of his more fanatical followers would like to admit. We are told that he was found by his wife Hafsa with a Coptic slave from whom he had promised to separate. Hafsa told A'isha, another of Mohammad's wives. Under the lash of both women's anger Mohammad sought to free himself from his promises by presenting the Koranic chapter, 'Prohibition' (lxvi). He evaded their anger and neatly turned Hafsa and A'isha into the offenders: 'If you two turn to Allah in repentance (for your hearts have sinned) you shall be pardoned; but if you conspire against him [Mohammad] know that Allah is his protector, and Gabriel and the righteous among the faithful. The angels too are his helpers. It may well be that, if he divorce you, his Lord will give him better wives than yourselves, submissive to Allah and full of faith, devout, penitent, obedient and given to fasting; both widows and virgins.'

The Koranic selections which follow are representative of

* My italics.

Islamic attitudes in the light of our contemporary need to understand them.*

'We created man of a sperm-drop, a mingling, trying him; and We made him hearing, seeing. Surely we guided him upon the way whether he be grateful or thankless. Surely have we prepared for the unbelievers chains, fetters, and a Blaze.' Sura lxxvi: 'Man'.

'I swear by all that you can see, and all that is hidden from your view, that this is the utterance of a noble messenger. It is no poet's speech: scant is your faith! It is no soothsayer's divination: how little you reflect! It is a revelation from the Lord of all creatures.' Sura lvi: 'The Inevitable'.

'When the earth shakes and quivers and the mountains crumble away and scatter into fine dust, you shall be divided into three multitudes: those on the right (blessed shall be those on the right!); those on the left (damned shall be those on the left!); and those to the fore (foremost shall be those!). Such are they that shall be brought near to their Lord in the gardens of delight; a whole multitude from the men of old but only a few from later generations.

'They shall recline on jewelled couches face to face, and there shall wait on them immortal youths with bowls and ewers and a cup of purest wine (that will neither pain their heads nor take away their reason); with fruits of their own choice and flesh of fowls. . . . And theirs shall be the dark-eyed houris, chaste as hidden pearls; a guerdon for their deeds. There they shall hear no idle talk, no sinful speech. . . .

'Those on the right hand . . . shall recline on couches raised high in the shade of thornless sidrahs and clusters of talh; amidst gushing waters and abundant fruits, unforbidden, never-ending. We created the houris and made them virgins, loving

---

* I am grateful to a renowned Islamic scholar for these translations; he insists on anonymity 'because collaboration with an unbeliever would be disapproved by many of my colleagues'. Generally, the translations conform with those made by Arberry and Dawood.

companions for those on the right hand; a multitude from the men of old and a multitude from the later generations.

'Those on the left hand . . . shall dwell amidst scorching winds and seething water. . . .' Ibid.

'On that day [Day of Judgment] the heavens shall become like molten brass and the mountains like tufts of wool scattered in the wind. Friends will meet, but shall not speak. To redeem himself from the torment of that day the sinner will gladly sacrifice his children, his wife, his brother, the kinsfolk who gave him shelter and all the people of the earth, if this might deliver him.' Sura lxx: 'The Ladders'.

'The worshippers, those who care for the needy, who believe in the Day of Reckoning and dread the punishment of their Lord, who restrain their carnal desire (save with their wives and slave-girls, for these are lawful to them: he that lusts after other than these is a transgressor). Those who keep their trusts . . . and attend promptly to their prayers . . . these shall be laden with honours and shall dwell in fair gardens.' Ibid.

'This is the Paradise which the righteous have been promised: it is watered by running streams, it has eternal fruits, and eternal shades. Such is the reward of the righteous, But the reward of the unbelievers is the fire of Hell.' Sura xiii: 'Thunder'.

'Shall I tell you on whom the devils descend? They descend on every lying sinner. They eagerly listen but most of them are liars. Poets are followed by none save erring men. See how aimlessly they rove in every valley, preaching what they never practise.' Sura xxvi: 'The Poets'.

'Recite your prayers at sunset, at nightfall and at dawn; the dawn prayer has its witnesses. Pray during the night as well, an additional duty for the fulfilment of which your Lord may exalt you to an honourable station.' Ibid.

'Say: "Praise be to Allah who has never begotten a son, who has no partner in his kingdom; who needs none to defend him from humiliation." ' Sura xvii: 'The Night Journey'.

'Allah does not forbid you to be kind and equitable to those who have neither made war on your religion nor driven you from their homes. . . . But he forbids you to make friends with those who have fought against you because of your religion and driven you from your homes and abetted others to do so. Those that make friends with them are wrongdoers.' Sura lx: 'She Who is Tested'.

'Believers, when believing women seek refuge with you, test them. . . . If you find them true believers do not return them to the infidels; they are not lawful to the infidels. . . . But hand back to the unbelievers the dowries they gave them. Nor is it an offence for you to marry such women. . . . Do not hold on to your marriage with unbelieving women. . . .' Ibid.

'Allah has promised you rich booty and has given you this [originally, the spoils taken at the battle of Khayber] with all promptness. He has protected you from your enemies, so that he may make your victory a sign to true believers and guide you along a straight path.' Sura xlviii: 'Victory'.

'No soul shall bear another's burden. To Allah you shall all return and He will declare to you what you have done. He knows your inmost thoughts.' Sura xxxix: 'The Hordes'.

'We said to Job: "Take a bunch of twigs and beat your wife with it; do not break your oath." We found him full of patience. He was a good and faithful man.' Sura xxxviii: 'Sad'. [Job had sworn to give his wife one hundred blows. The oath was kept by his giving her one blow with a bunch of a hundred twigs. Koranic scholars quote this passage as permitting any similar release from an oath rashly taken.]

'Kill them [the aggressors] wherever you find them. Drive them out of the places from which they drove you. Idolatry is worse than carnage. But do not fight them in the precincts of the Holy Mosque unless they attack you there; if they attack you put them to the sword. . . . Fight against them until Allah's religion is supreme.' Sura ii: 'The Cow'.

'Make the pilgrimage in the appointed months. He that intends to perform it in those months must abstain from sexual intercourse, obscene language and acrimonious disputes while on pilgrimage.' Ibid.

'You shall not wed pagan women. . . . A believing slave girl is better than an idolatress, although she may please you. . . . Keep aloof from women during their menstrual periods and do not touch them until they are clean again. Then have intercourse with them as Allah enjoined you. Women are your fields; go then into your fields as you please. Do good works and fear Allah. . . .' Ibid.

'You are forbidden to take in marriage married women, except captive slaves. Such is the decree of Allah. All women other than these are lawful to you, provided you seek them with your wealth in modest conduct. . . . As a duty give them their dowry for the enjoyment you have had of them, but it shall be no offence to make any other arrangement among yourselves after you have fulfilled your duty.' Sura iv: 'Women'.

'. . . We stirred among them [Christians] enmity and hatred, which shall endure until the Day of Resurrection. . . . As for the unbelievers, if they offered all that the earth contains and as much besides to redeem themselves from the torment of the Day of Resurrection it shall not be accepted from them. Theirs shall be a woeful punishment.' Sura v: 'The Table'.

'As for the man or women who is guilty of theft, cut off their hands to punish them for their crimes.' Ibid.

'You cannot help a man if Allah seeks to mislead him. Those whose hearts he does not please to purify shall be rewarded with disgrace in this world and grievous punishment in the next.' Ibid.

'Believers, take neither Jews nor Christians for friends. They are friends with one another. Whoever of you seeks their friendship shall become one of their number.' Ibid.

'Allah will not punish you for that which is inadvertent in your oaths.' Ibid.

'Believers, you are accountable for none but yourselves; he that goes astray cannot harm you if you are on the right path.' Ibid.

'Permission to take up arms is hereby given to those who are attacked. . . . Allah has power to grant them victory.' Sura xxii: 'Pilgrimage'.

'Fight for the cause of Allah with the devotion due to him. He has chosen you and imposed on you no burdens in the observance of your faith. . . . In this as in former scriptures he has given you the name of Moslems, so that his apostle may testify against you [should you default in any way], and that you yourselves may testify against your fellowmen [non-Moslems, all of whom are defaulters].' Ibid.

'Men are tempted by the love of lusts—the lure of women and offspring, of hoarded treasures of gold and silver, of splendid horses, cattle and cornfields. These are the comforts of this life, but far better is the return to Allah.' Sura iii: 'The Imrans'.

'Allah is the supreme Plotter.' Ibid.

'Believers, fear Allah as you rightly should, and when death comes, die true Moslems. Cling one and all to the faith of Allah and let nothing divide you.' Ibid.

'Believers, do not make friends with any men other than your own people. They will corrupt you. They desire nothing but your ruin. Their hatred is clear from what they say, but more violent is the hatred concealed in their breasts.' Ibid.

'If you have suffered a defeat so did the enemy. We alternate these vicissitudes among mankind so that Allah may know true believers and choose martyrs from among you . . . and that He may test the faithful and annihilate the infidels.' Ibid.

'If you should die or be slain in the cause of Allah his forgiveness and His mercy would surely be better than all the riches they [the infidels] amass.' Ibid.

'Who is more wicked than the man who invents a falsehood about Allah, or says, "This has been revealed to me", when nothing has been revealed to him? Or the man who says, "I can reveal the like of what Allah has revealed"?' Sura vi: 'Cattle'.

In the Mohammadan conception of Allah, the attributes of mercy and love are overshadowed by those of majesty, awe and vengeance. The terrors of Judgment Day so powerfully described in the Koran were believed and are still believed with an intensity of conviction which is difficult for Westerners to understand.

Nicholson notes that, 'The Koran generally represents Allah as a stern, unapproachable despot, requiring utter submission to His arbitrary will, but infinitely unconcerned with human feelings and aspirations.'

In about twenty years Mohammad sowed the seeds of almost every development which occurs in the political and intellectual history of the Arabs during the ages to come. More than any man in history Mohammad shaped the destinies of his people and down the centuries they looked back to him for guidance and authority at each step.

Islamic legal commands are incorporated in the Koran, which is the constitution and the bill of rights of the Islamic state. These laws are infallible. Man can only obey them, and in his attempt to consummate his obedience to these commands he realizes his religious ideal. Accordingly, law in Islam has the character of a *religious obligation*. At the same time it constitutes a political sanction of religion.

These laws are divine and cannot be altered. By its very nature Allah's word must be considered final. Although Allah is known to have changed his mind a certain number of times, abrogating specific injunctions given his Prophet and replacing them by equally good or better ones, organic change of Moslem law stopped at the death of Mohammad.

Mohammad founded a religious and political system that revolutionized Arab society and sanctioned violence as a principal means to a great end—nothing less than world domination by force.

But the greatest irony of Islam is the nature of Mohammad himself. The active career of the prophet began in highway robbery in the month then consecrated in Arabia to unbroken peace. He elevated plunder to a religious act; he butchered captives all through a day, completing the task by torchlight, and took that night Rihana, a Jewish captive girl, as his bond-slave; he debased the Arab code of purity and honour—a code which itself permitted polygamy and brigandage—by marrying a captive woman Safia three days after the death of her relatives, by committing incest in making his adopted son divorce his wife and immediately marrying her himself, and by robbing pilgrims on their way to Mecca. He then proclaimed divine suras declaring these acts to be the will of Allah.*

The grip which Mohammad and the Koran still have on many Moslems is shown in much modern writing.

In 1973 Halid-i Baghdadi was telling his readers that

'For the vicious and for disbelievers there is torment in their graves. This is certainly to be believed. A dead person, when put into his grave, will come to life with an unknown life. He will be either at ease or in torment. Two angels named Munker and Nekir disguised in two unknown, horrible persons will come to his grave and question him. These facts are declared clearly in hadiths. The questions in the grave will be on some of the principles [of Islam]. . . . For this reason, we should teach our children the answers of the following questions:

'Who is your Rab [master]? (The answer, of course, is "Allah".) What is your religion? Whose people are you of? What is your holy book? What is your direction? [i.e. in what direction do you turn when praying? The answer is "Mecca".] What is your sect in worship? It is written that those who are not true Moslems will not answer correctly.

* As Professor W. H. T. Gairdner has said: 'As incidents in the life of an Arab conqueror, the tales of raiding, private assassinations and public executions, perpetual enlargements of the harem, and so forth, might be historically explicable and therefore pardonable; but it is another matter that they should be taken as a setting forth of the moral ideal for all time.'

'The graves of those who give precise answer will enlarge. A window will be opened to Paradise. Every morning and every evening they will see their places in Paradise. Angels will do them favours and give them good news. He who can not answer beautifully will be beaten with iron mallets so severely that every creature but mankind and genies will hear him cry out. His grave will become so tight that he will feel as if his bones would intertwine. A hole will be opened to Hell. In the morning and in the evening he will see his place in Hell. He will be tormented bitterly in his grave till Resurrection.'*

With the abjurations of the Koran and of Koranic scholars so unequivocal and severe it is not surprising that Islam is so powerful and that theologians exercise such profound influence and promise such extreme punishments. Islamic attitudes to punishment were set out by Sheikh Mohammad Abu Zahra, a member of the Academy of Islamic Research at the fourth conference of the Academy, Cairo, 1968: 'Let it be known that Islam is the law of the Moslem state. Whoever trifles with it, whether he be a Moslem or otherwise is only seeking to upset the organic law of the state. It is right that the state should protect its system with the most severe penalties, seeing that an apostate is a rebel against the state who deserves the utmost punishment.'

Sheikh Zahra noted that 'to kiss or hug a girl is a crime since it paves the way for adultery, though it is a less serious crime than adultery itself, being only a means to an end'. He warned Moslems against 'the sin of seeing a woman's pudenda, a matter prohibited by law'. The most serious crime, he stressed, is apostasy and punishment for it was instituted by tradition: 'Whoever changes his religion put him to death.' He quoted another tradition in support: 'It is unlawful to shed a Moslem's blood except for adultery, life for life and apostasy.'

The Sheikh concluded, 'The punishment has been bitterly

* *Belief and Islam*, published in Istanbul.

criticized by those who circulate malicious reports about Islam, alleging that it is incompatible with religious freedom. These are warped critics; no one who professes a faith would think of abjuring it unless he discovers the falsity of its tenets. Islam being based on true tenets, no believer ever thinks of rejecting it except under compulsion.'

The influence of the Koran cannot be over-emphasized. It is known to the least educated people and even to illiterates because it has for centuries been the main text in the village schools, and in weekly 'sermons' in the mosque. Ordinary conversation includes many references to Allah, Mohammad and Koranic verse, as well as suggestions, plans, and advice culled from the Koran, and appeal to Koranic and other proverbs for justification. To ward off the bad influence of jinns and evil spirits many people, especially in Saudi Arabia, employ readers to come to their houses and recite parts of the Koran every evening for about two hours, between the sunset and evening prayers.

A popular treatment for many chronic ailments, particularly nervous ones, is to write a chapter from the Koran on a plate, pour plain water or rose-water on this so as to dissolve the writing, and then give the patient the water to drink. Quacks in Bahrein and Kuwait find this kind of 'treatment' most profitable. A similar remedy, popular for chronic ulcers, is for a relative of the patient to stand at the door of the Mosque with a cup of water, or clarified butter, into which each member of the congregation breathes as he comes out, some in addition reading a verse or two of the Koran or reciting a prayer for the patient's recovery. The contents of the cup are then drunk by the patient.

A short novel in 1970 by the Egyptian writer Yahya Haqqi relates the difficulties of a young Egyptian doctor returning home on completion of his studies in England. He loves his country but 'the more his love for Egypt grew, the more he became exasperated with the Egyptians' and their refusal to accept beneficial change. The young doctor is infuriated by the superstitious beliefs of the people but his outbursts against customary beliefs provoke violent opposition. He still hopes to prove the superiority of his modern techniques over the customary, superstitious way by effecting a dramatic success with his first patient. But he fails. The young doctor is about to lose his self-confidence but then realizes that 'there is no science without faith'. He makes his peace, outwardly at least, with the customary beliefs. This restores the people's confidence in him and he resumes the treatment of his first patient, this time with success. The happy end of the story is that the doctor continues to practise medicine in his native region, 'relying on Allah as well as on his science and his hands'.

The story is an object lesson for modernizers: new techniques can be successfully introduced if they are not presented as opposed to traditional beliefs. It also reveals that although the Western-educated professional may be accepted by the people on a practical basis, his world view remains alien and incomprehensible.

3 *The Child of Customs*

'If it were not for the almost ceaseless wars and feuds, Arabia would probably be one of the most populous countries in the world.' Sheikh Hafiz Wahba, *Arabian Days*, 1964.

'Nothing can befall us but what Allah hath destined.' Koran, sura x, 51.

'Men have no control over their destinies.' Koran, sura liv, 49.

The first crisis in Islam came immediately on the death of the Prophet in 632. Mohammad had never claimed to be more than mortal man, though distinguished above others because he was Allah's messenger and spokesman. But he had left no clear instructions on who was to succeed him as leader of the Islamic community and ruler of the new-born Islamic state. After argument, the Moslems agreed to appoint Abu Bakr as *khalifa* (deputy) of the Prophet—thus creating the great historical tradition of the Caliphate.

It also created a second tradition—regicide. Of the four Caliphs who followed the Prophet as head of the Islamic community, three (and possibly all four) were murdered. Two of these were struck down by mutineers and fanatics who saw themselves as heroes freeing the community from wicked rulers.

A civil war followed the Caliph Uthman's death. Mu'awiya, governor of Syria and kinsman of the murdered Caliph, demanded that the killers be punished. Ali, who had succeeded Uthman, did nothing and his supporters claimed that no crime had been committed. Since Uthman had been an oppressor, his death, they said, was an execution, not a murder. A few years later Ali himself was murdered and the same argument was used by the Kharijite sect responsible.

The Kharijites, with a fierce spirit of fanaticism moulding their religious views, were gloomy and austere, as befitted the chosen few in an ungodly world. The Koran ruled their lives and possessed their imaginations, so that the history of the early Islamic church, the persecutions, martyrdoms and triumphs of the Faith became a drama enacted by themselves. Their fear of hell kindled an inquisitorial zeal for righteousness. They examined everybody's belief and woe to him who was found at fault. A single false step involved excommunication from Islam and though the slip might be condoned on proof of sincere repentance—or, later, a visit to Mecca*—any Moslem who had once committed a mortal sin was held to be inevitably damned with the infidels in everlasting fire.

In the last years of Mohammad's life it had been a pious custom that when two Moslems met one would ask for news (hadith) of the Prophet and the other should relate a saying or an anecdote. After his death the custom continued and the word 'hadith' was applied to sayings and stories which were no longer new. In time an elaborate system of tradition was built up to supplement the Koran which was found insufficient for the complicated needs of a rapidly extending ideology. During the first century of Islam there were numerous living witnesses from whom traditions were collected, committed to memory and orally handed down. As Nicholson expresses it: 'Every tradition consists of two parts: the text (matn) and the authority (sanad or isnad), e.g. the relater says, "I was told by A, who was informed by B, who had it from C, that the Prophet (God bless him!) . . . used to open prayer with the words 'Praise to God, the Lord of all creatures'."'

This then became the practice for all Moslems. The forging of traditions became a recognized political and religious weapon

* Since a pilgrimage to Mecca automatically wins pardon for sins already committed and any that may be committed in the future, this, in effect, confers immunity on the pilgrim. So those Moslems who have not been to Mecca shun, in self-defence, those who have made the pilgrimage.

and all parties used it. Even men of strict piety insisted that the end justified the fraud and they used words supposedly spoken by Mohammad to support their point of view: 'You must compare the sayings attributed to me with the Koran; what agrees therewith is from me, whether I actually said it or no.' And again: 'Whatever good saying has been said, I myself have said it.' As the result of such elastic principles every new doctrine took the form of an apostolic hadith; every sect and every system defended itself by an appeal to the authority of Mohammad. When Bukhari drew up his collection of hadiths in A.D. 870—he entitled it *The Genuine*—he limited it to about 7,000—selected from 600,000.

Islam needed a code or holy law and it was found in the Shari'a, developed by jurists from the Koran and the traditions of the Prophet. The Shari'a was not only a normative code of law but also, socially and politically, a pattern of conduct, an ideal towards which Islam expects men and society to strive. The 'divinely granted' Shari'a regulated every aspect of life, not only belief and cult, but also public law, constitutional and international, and private law, criminal and civil.*

Islamic legal doctrine does not rest on the basis of protecting the individual against the State. The jurists subordinate the principle of individual liberty to that of the public interest and welfare. Under this ideal form of government, they argue, all men will naturally receive their due rights. The supreme paradox, which nullifies this pious ideal, lies in the Shari'a's failure to provide any guarantee that government will, in practice, assume this ideal form; far from ensuring the existence of practical remedies against the ruler's abuse of his recognized powers, it simply counsels acceptance of such abuse.

From the beginning the Shari'a identified right action and laid down precise worldly penalties for doing wrong. To uphold the Shari'a and impose the penalties, to watch over the per-

* Abdullah, later to be King of Jordan, explained to T. E. Lawrence that, when appropriate, the Arabs would 'discover' in the Koran such opinions and judgments as were required to make it suitable for modern commercial operations, like banking and exchange.

formance of all duties commanded by God, to spread the bounds of the faith by holy war (jihad)—all these involved a leader with political power. Thus the Islamic community could not be complete unless it was also a State, and political action was a way of serving God. 'It is a duty to consider the exercise of power as one of the forms of religion, as one of the acts by which man draws near God.'*

It is interesting at this point to contrast Christianity with Mohammadanism. Christianity came into being as a religion of the oppressed and persecuted minority in a mighty empire; the State regarded them as a hostile element and they repudiated it. Islam, however, came into being as a movement founding a state, establishing a policy of its own, as a triumphant force conquering countries as much as winning souls.

There is a further, still more significant distinction: Islam is a religion of pride so humiliations impinge themselves on to the religion; Christianity is an ideology of humility so blows against pride have no effect.

Again, Islam may proclaim that Allah is generous and merciful. But it does not, like Judaism and Christianity, proclaim that men are His children. They are His slaves and His subjects.

Largely because of varying interpretations of Islamic law factional strife was soon rife. In 813 a new Caliph, al-Ma'mun, came to power after a bitter civil war in which he defeated his brother, the previous Caliph al-Amin. Before al-Ma'mun could take direct control of Baghdad, local forces, still in opposition to him, were terrorizing the populace. In response, local vigilance groups were organized to protect the people against banditry and assaults. A man named Khalid al-Daryush mobilized his neighbours and the people of his quarter to fight the thieves and bandits, using the religious slogan, 'Command the Good and Forbid the Evil'.

This slogan had far-reaching effects in the Moslem religious mentality. Every Moslem was obliged not only to obey the

* Ibn Taymiyya, *al-Siyasa.*

49

legal, moral and ritual teachings of Islam, but to prevent the gross violation of these precepts by others. Islamic religious sentiment was essentially communal, and the salvation, or right ordering, of the community as a whole was as essential a religious duty as individual conformity to the holy law. By employing this slogan Khalid appealed to a broader concern than self-interested protection against violence and racketeering; he tried to mobilize the latent religious sentiment which made each Moslem personally responsible for a just society. Indeed Khalid was appealing to a sentiment akin to that which ignites jihad.

For centuries a holy war of kinds was waged by the Assassins, forerunners of today's terrorists. The name was given to a murderous group of Syrian Moslems led by a mysterious prophet known as the Old Man of the Mountain. The word 'assassin' first appears in the chronicles of the Crusades, but the writers did not then know that the Old Man had established a remarkable haven for his followers in the fortress and valley of Alamut, headquarters of the sect for centuries. He had enclosed the valley and turned it into a beautiful garden with every variety of fruit. Its elegant palaces and pavilions were gilded and covered with exquisite painting. Runnels flowed freely with wine and milk and honey and water, and women said to be the most beautiful in the world played music, sang sweetly and danced seductively. The Old Man wanted to make his people believe that this really *was* paradise, so he fashioned it after Mohammad's paradise. Here the young Assassins indulged themselves in every pleasure until the Old Man needed their services. Then a young man would be taken to the 'Prophet' who would ask him from whence he came.

'From Paradise,' was the sincere answer.

'Go then and slay a man I shall name,' the Old Man would command. 'When you return my angels shall bear thee again to Paradise. And should you die, nevertheless they will carry you to Paradise.'

The young men so manipulated would do anything their

Master asked them, if only to get back to the delights of 'paradise'. The superlative skill of the Assassins in disguise and murder and their fanaticism and devotion reached European ears through the descriptions by such travellers as Marco Polo and Odoric of Pordenone.

The Assassins belonged to the Isma'ili sect, a dissident sect and an offshoot of the Shi'a group, whose quarrel with the Sunnis was the major religious schism in Islam. The enemy, for the Isma'ilis, was the Sunni establishment—political and military, bureaucratic and religious. Their murders were designed to frighten, to weaken and ultimately to overthrow it. In a calculated war of terror, the Assassins brought death to sovereigns, princes, generals, governors and even divines who had condemned Isma'ili doctrines. 'To kill these people is more lawful than rainwater,' said one Assassin leader. 'To shed the blood of a heretic is more meritorious than to kill seventy Greek infidels.'

The ancient Assassins were as inescapable as their modern counterparts. In 1108 they killed Ubayd Allal al-Khatib, a chief of Isfahan, and an enemy of the Isma'ilis. Ubayd wore armour and had a loyal bodyguard but an Assassin struck him down at prayers in a mosque.

Assassin tactics were simple and direct. They seized or bought fortresses for use as bases in a campaign of terror. To this end, they tried to subvert and direct the zeal of the faithful Moslems, especially in mountainous areas; also, they made discreet alliances with princes when expediency dictated. The Assassins achieved such influence that even in Damascus itself they were given a building—supposedly a palace—as a headquarters.

The Assassins had a complex organization, with agents in many towns, so that an agent on a mission could travel across Iraq and Syria without the need to meet strangers who might report him to officials.

A startling story is told by the brother of the great Saladin so feared by the Crusaders. Rashid al-Din, the Assassin leader, sent a courier to Saladin and ordered him to deliver his message only in private. Saladin had the man searched but nothing dangerous was found so the great man dismissed his assembly except for his two highly trusted Mameluke guards. He then ordered the agent to deliver the message.

He replied, 'I have been ordered to deliver it in private.'

'These two men do not leave me,' said Saladin. 'Deliver your message or go.'

'As you sent the others away why do you not dismiss these two men?' the messenger asked.

'Because I regard them as my own sons and they and I are as one,' Saladin said.

The messenger turned to the Mamelukes. 'If I ordered you in the name of my master Rashid al-Din to kill this Sultan would you do so?'

They drew their swords and said, 'Command as you wish.' While Saladin sat astounded the messenger left, taking the two Mamelukes with him. Saladin apparently discerned Rashid al-Din's more subtle message, for he made friendly arrangements with him.

In one respect, as Professor Bernard Lewis has pointed out, the Assassins have no precedent—in the planned, systematic and long-term use of terror as a political weapon. Previous political murders were the work of individuals or small groups of plotters. Certainly in the 'skills' of murder and conspiracy the Assassins had many predecessors but they could well have been the first terrorists. They showed that the Islamic state with autocratic, centralized power based on personal and transient loyalties is acutely vulnerable to terrorism and assassination, for Islamic tradition recognizes the principle of justifiable revolt. Since no procedure exists to test the righteousness of a command or to exercise the right to disobey one that is sinful, the conscientious subject may rebel against the ruler and try to depose him. Another course, more expeditious, is to assassinate him.

This vulnerability of Moslem leaders exists today. Nowhere is political assassination more frequent than in the Arab world.

An example is the murder of the Jordanian Prime Minister, Wasfi el-Tel, by Palestinian terrorists in Cairo in 1972. The Egyptians saw this as an 'execution' and after a time in prison the killers were quietly released. On the same principle, the five assassins who killed thirty-two people at Athens airport in January 1974 were later 'arrested' by their own people but the Arab world—if not the Western countries—knew that no severe punishment would follow.

Other kinds of violence were being done to the Faith throughout the tenth to twelfth centuries. Discrepancy between Moslem theory of state and the administration of political power had early become apparent. In political organization as well as in the administration of the law the gap between the dreams and the actual conduct of state was wide. Bribery condoned injustice; judges were often in collusion with those in power to convict the innocent. 'Unprotected against executive transgression, the administration of the law not infrequently broke down altogether.'*

Moslems were aware of the corruption and oppression under which they were living but they clung tenaciously to their concept of rulership. By the eleventh century, the ruthless realities were too flagrant to be overlooked. The disappointment was immense and the defeat was acknowledged openly by most believers. The requirements of legitimate power had to be redefined with ever greater leniency, until the low had been reached and the theoretical dream abandoned. Whoever had power was obeyed by the Arab, who thought it his obligation to do so in order that the religious community would continue. Anything was better than anarchy. With disillusionment and cynicism the Arab viewed political life; his state of feelings was that of utter hopelessness and resignation.†

After eight centuries there is less hopelessness but even more resignation.

Next to Mohammad himself, the Arab who has exercised

---

* Michel Feghali, *Proverbes et dictons syro-libanais*, 1938.
† Michel Feghali, op. cit.

most influence on the Islamic world is Ibn Khaldun (1332–1406). Educated Arabs—and these are the ones who manipulate the semi-educated who in turn manipulate the masses—are more prone to quote Khaldun than Mohammad. His book, *The Muqaddimah—An Introduction to History*, is a window on Arab life and thought. Born in Tunis, tutored in the Koran and hadith-literature, in jurisprudence and the subtleties of Arabic poetry and grammar by some of the best scholars of his time, Khaldun was to become one of the great Arab philosophers and statesmen. He finished his *Muqaddimah* in 1377 and later held important academic and political posts in Cairo, where he died. His book is the earliest attempt made by any historian to discover a pattern in the changes that occur in man's political and social organization. Khaldun illustrates his theories by events and episodes in world history, particularly Arab history, sometimes giving two, three or even more illustrations to support a single point.

His first words are: 'In the name of Allah, the Compassionate, the Merciful. Pray, O Allah, for our master, Mohammad, his family and the men around him.' His devotion to the teachings of the Master are evident throughout the *Muqaddimah*, and indirectly and directly he represented them for Islamic posterity. 'One feels shame,' he writes, 'when one's relatives are treated unjustly or attacked, and one wishes to intervene between them and whatever peril or destruction threatens them.' And again: 'The affection everybody has for his allies results from the feeling of shame that comes to a person when one of his neighbours, relatives or a blood relation in any degree is humiliated. . . . One must understand Mohammad's remark, "Learn as much of your pedigrees as is necessary to establish your ties of kindred."' He is only one of thousands of Arab writers to dwell on shame and humiliation.

For Khaldun no human being could exist who possesses an unbroken pedigree of nobility from Adam down to himself —except Mohammad. His pedigree was a special act of divine grace as 'a measure designed to safeguard his true character'.

Khaldun knew his people's weaknesses and obliquely chided them. 'Many leaders of tribes or groups are eager to acquire certain pedigrees. They desire them because persons of that particular descent possessed some special virtue, such as bravery or nobility, or fame, however this may have come about. They go after such a family and involve themselves in claims to belong to a branch of it. These pedigrees are invented by people to get into the good graces of rulers through sycophantic behaviour. . . .'

Good rulership, said Khaldun, is equivalent to mildness. He regretted that mildness was seldom seen. 'If the ruler uses force and is ready to mete out punishment and is eager to expose the faults of people and to count their sins, his subjects become fearful and depressed and seek to protect themselves against him through lies, ruses and deceit. This becomes a character trait of theirs. Their mind and character become corrupted. They often abandon the ruler on the battlefield and fail to support his defensive enterprises. The decay of sincere intentions causes the decay of the military protection. The subjects often conspire to kill their ruler. Thus the dynasty decays. . . .'

It should be known, Khaldun explained, that both 'the sword' and 'the pen' are instruments for the ruler to use. However, at the beginning of a dynasty the need for the sword is greater than that for the pen. In that situation (with the people intent upon establishing power) the pen is merely a servant and agent of the ruler's authority. The same is the case at the end of a dynasty when its group feeling weakens. The dynasty then needs the support of the military.

As with nearly all Arab philosophers, Khaldun was ambivalent about force for he too was obsessed with jihad and the rights of a leader. 'Rarely will a human being concede perfection and superiority to another unless he is somehow forced to do so by superior strength,' he observed, unconscious of irony. He reminded his readers that Mohammad had only censured wrathfulness that was 'in the service of Satan'. But righteous anger was 'the ability to help the truth become victorious'.

Without it 'there would no longer be Holy War . . .' and this was a religious duty because of the universality of the Moslem mission and the obligation to convert everybody to Islam either by persuasion or by force.

The significance of Khaldun's writings on this point, underscoring Mohammad's preaching, cannot be over-emphasized. The concept of universal Islamic overlordship and the failure to execute it despite many centuries of effort are paramount thought-threads in the Arab mind.

Once again, the Koran was the basis of Khaldun's understanding because its language indicated all the requirements of all situations, whether they were stated or understood. In addition, the Koran was perfect in choice of words and excellence of arrangement and combination. 'This is its inimitability, a quality that surpasses comprehension.'

Khaldun is much to blame for the terrible weakness of Arab education—learning by rote rather than by reason. He taught teachers

'not to ask more from a student than that he understand the book he is engaged in studying, in accordance with his class [age group] and his receptivity to instruction, whether he is at the start or at the end of his studies. The teacher should not bring in problems other than those found in that particular book, until the student knows the whole [book] from beginning to end, is acquainted with its purpose, and has gained a habit from it, which he then can apply to other [books]. When the student has acquired the scholarly habit [knowledge by memory] in one discipline, he is prepared for learning all the others. He also has become interested in looking for more and in advancing to higher learning. Thus, he eventually acquires a complete mastery of scholarship. But if a teacher confuses a student, he will be unable to understand. He becomes indolent and stops thinking. He despairs of becoming a scholar and avoids scholarship and instruction'.

At the same time, Khaldun, more pragmatically, reminded his readers of the old Arab proverb that 'Many a trick is worth more than a tribe.'

Western sociology has rediscovered Ibn Khaldun and finds in him evidence of sociological concepts such as 'solidarity'. But ironically, contemporary *Arabic* thought about Khaldun is beginning to sour. For instance, Ishaq Musa al-Husayni, a Palestinian living in Cairo, has criticized '. . . our obsession with the past and the respect bordering on worship, for ancient laws, repeating all the while this vague and magical incantation, "We can remedy the present only with the remedies of the past." This, in effect, means that we must go back to the deserts and caves, ride on camels, wear our traditional baggy robes, treat diseases by cauterization, allow epidemics to decimate us, content ourselves by reading incantations. . . .'*

Khaldun preached solidarity in views which President Nasser and other Arab leaders have echoed ad nauseam. He also clearly stated why no solidarity was possible, in views which Nasser and the others have ignored. 'The Arabs are incapable of founding an empire unless they are imbued with religious enthusiasm by a prophet or saint.'

Six hundred years later Albert Hourani† could see Khaldun's 'solidarity' more objectively but no less emphatically. 'For Moslems no sort of natural solidarity, not even patriotism, can replace the bond created by Islam. Real unity, in a Moslem nation, rests on common religious conviction. If that goes, society itself dissolves.'

Even more pertinently, Hourani sees the awful handicaps facing the Arabs with 'stagnation and slavish imitation, the characteristic ills of traditional Islam. . . .' He refers particularly to Islam's foundation on the pursuit of domination and power and strength and might and the refusal to recognize any law which is contrary to the Shari'a and its divine law.

* *The Crisis in Arab Thought*, Beirut, 1954.
† Reader in the Modern History of the Near East, Oxford University, and Fellow of St Antony's College.

Whatever Hourani's emotions in the twentieth century, those displayed by Khaldun in the fourteenth were sad and nostalgic for he knew that in the eleventh century the world of Islam, after a long period of weakening, had been in a state of manifest decay which quickened when Islam was attacked by enemies on all sides—and from within. In Europe, Christian forces wrested territory from the Moslems in Spain and Sicily; in Africa the Berbers took most of north-west Africa and the parts of Spain which had remained under Arab rule. Libya and Tunisia were devastated by other forces. From Central Asia came the greatest danger of all—the Turks; they were to become supreme in Cairo and to have the most permanent effect of all the Moslems' enemies. The first Crusaders arrived in 1096. An early experiment in imperialism, the Crusaders were to leave an ineradicable mark on Islam. In the East, Ghengis Khan began the Mongol conquest which culminated in the seizure of Persia and Iraq. Islam was totally humiliated. And, with the further humiliations which were to follow down the centuries, Islam was not to begin to recover until it won the opening 'battles' of the Oil War which began in 1973.

Some important aspects of Islam need explanation. For instance, Westerners frequently ask why the Arabs have not been able to change as other peoples have changed; even the Chinese, an introverted people, have progressed. The Arabs' difficulty is that Islam has always been rigidly traditionalist.* The examples to be followed belong to the ever more remote past. Mohammad's followers were the best generation, their successors the second best. From then on the world has been deteriorating and deterioration will continue until the world comes to its ordained end. The living generation is prohibited from changing the inherited ways—for change can only be for the worse. Innovation is rejected, the innovator is liable to punishment.

* Arabs know their own attachment to tradition. To the four 'natures' into which Arab physiologists used to divide human character—the choleric, bilious, melancholy, and phlegmatic—a popular saying adds another: 'Custom', it is said, 'is a fifth nature'. Most Arabs do not know it but the maxim echoes Khaldun who had said, 'Man is the child of customs, not the child of his ancestors.'

58

The reformer has only two courses: he adduces prophetic or koranic witness for his proposal or advocates the return to the 'golden age' of primitive Islam. Reformer or iconoclast, the Arab is always appealing to Allah.

Lawrence observes that the Arabs he knew 'felt no incongruity in bringing God into the weaknesses and appetites of their least creditable causes. He was the most familiar of their words. . . .'

For a long time Western writers described Islam as a 'sensual' religion, presumably because the Koran permits a man to take as many as four wives. Richard Burton, the great nineteenth-century traveller and orientalist who knew Arab Moslem life intimately, protested against this kind of misunderstanding. 'Can we call that faith sensual which forbids a man to look upon a statue or a picture? Which condemns even the most moderate use of inebriants, and is not certain upon the subject of coffee and tobacco? Which will not allow even the most harmless game of chance or skill? Which vigorously prohibits music, dancing, and even poetry and works of fiction upon any but strictly religious subjects? Above all things, which debars man from the charms of female society, making sinful a glance at a strange woman's unveiled face? A religion whose votaries must pray five times a day at all seasons . . . ? Whose yearly fast [Ramadan] often becomes one of the severest trials to which the human frame can be exposed? To whom distant pilgrimage with all its trials and hardships is obligatory at least once in life?'

Burton was right in attacking the unfavourable stereotype, but the point is that in Islam both forbearance *and* indulgence are found in greater balance than in other religions familiar in the West. For instance, it is more indulgent towards sexual pleasure than either Christianity or Judaism. In requiring abstention during *daylight* for the whole month of Ramadan, the Koran (sura ii, 183) assures believers that they may 'approach' their wives each night. 'Now, therefore, go in unto them with full desire for that which God hath ordained for you.'

In the light of twentieth-century Western relations with the

59

Islamic world, perhaps the most important point is that Islamic tradition is not humanistic. This is not a denigration but simple fact. Islam does not regard the human form as a focal point, so human life is of no great consequence. What counts is obeying Allah. During the fourth Arab–Israeli war of 1973 President Sadat of Egypt shocked some Western people when he announced that he was willing to sacrifice 'hundreds of thousands' of Egyptian soldiers in the struggle. He meant it—and his statement was accepted by his people. Arabs no longer distinguish between a holy war and any other war—although the call to jihad still has great propaganda power—so that now all Moslems expect to go to Paradise if killed in battle.

Completely affirming political and military power, Islam gives a religious value to power, success and victory in themselves. Islam endows the army with the prestige and authority of an institution meriting divine blessing. Islam's heritage paves the way for military intervention which is regarded as most fitting and proper in the eyes of God and man.

Despite an undercurrent of liberal thought, Islam is in some ways more introverted than ever before, so that Moslems are rejecting Christians of their own race. This is tragically shown in an incident from the Yemen Civil War, 1962–5, in which Egyptian troops were involved. Two Egyptians, a Copt and a Moslem, both members of well-known and upper-class families, had been lifelong friends. They were wounded in the same action, the Moslem in the arm and the Copt in the leg. Disabled, they lay awaiting treatment and removal from the battlefield. A half-empty truck arrived and picked up the Moslem but left the Christian, despite his desperate pleas for help. The truck crew had orders to collect Moslems before Christians, but one word from the wounded Moslem could have saved the Copt. It was never uttered. The Copt died on the field, probably slaughtered by Yemeni tribesmen.*

* Moslems can usually identify a Christian, in the way that Catholics and Protestants in Northern Ireland can identify each other by physiognomy alone. The story is authentic beyond doubt but its source cannot be given here.

Impelled by Koranic exhortations and threats, imprisoned by Islamic traditions, victim of a society which holds life cheap and living in an environment where survival is difficult, it is not surprising that the Arab has a violent disposition, even less surprising that he can so readily find an excuse for violence.

The most dispassionate of Western scholars of Arab life, Doctor James Parkes, says, 'It was and still is the tragedy of Islam that all movements of reform suffer from a nostalgia for the simple life of the desert in which the faith was originally proclaimed, and have not found a way to make the teaching of its saints and mystics available to the life of the peasant and the townsman. . . . Islam has unhappily proved an agent for the division and degradation of the country, as much as for its enlightenment.'*

* *Whose Land?*, Pelican, 1971.

4 *Language and Literature*

Any explanation of the Arab mind must take into account the profound effect of language and literature on individuals and the whole Arab race. Albert Hourani, one of the greatest Arab scholars living in the West, has said that his people are more conscious of their language than any people in the world.

This 'consciousness' is obsessive. Language itself is an *act*. Even more, by saying that something is so, it *is* so. For instance, to say that an enemy is a murderer brings instant conviction that the man is a murderer; no proof is required. To claim to have inflicted heavy military losses on an enemy makes this a fact, even if no military action whatever took place. This is a difficult concept for a Westerner to grasp but until he does so many Arab actions and statements make little sense.

For instance, it is significant that in old Arabic the word *responsibility* (and its concept) are unknown. The word now

62

exists but in modern life one is never responsible; it is always the other party who is responsible. Similarly, the victim is always responsible for his own suffering. In the army an officer is never responsible and his men do not hold him so because, simply by the nature of things, authority carries no concomitant responsibility.

To understand the influence of language and literature it is necessary to go back to pre-Islamic days. The Koran is the oldest Arabic book but the beginnings of literary composition in the Arabic language can be traced back to an earlier period, before the art of writing was known. Probably all the pre-Islamic poems which have come down to us belong to the century preceding Islam (A.D. 500–622) and were committed to writing by Moslem scholars between 750 and 900.

Most Arabic-speaking Moslems have always regarded this poetry as a model of inimitable excellence. It was in the life of the people, it moulded their minds and fixed their character and made them morally and spiritually a nation long before Mohammad welded the various conflicting groups into a single organism. In those days poetry was no luxury for the cultured few, but the sole medium of literary expression. Every tribe had its poets, and their unwritten words 'flew across the desert faster than arrows', and in the midst of outward strife and disintegration they provided a unifying principle. Poetry gave life and currency to an ideal of Arabian virtue. Based on tribal community of blood and insisting that only ties of blood were sacred, it nevertheless became an invisible bond between diverse clans, and formed the basis of a national community of sentiment.

When a poet appeared in an Arab family neighbouring tribes about would gather together and wish the family joy. There would be feasts and the women would play lutes. The men and boys would congratulate one another; for a poet was a defence to the honour of them all, a weapon to ward off insult from their good name, and a means of perpetuating their glorious deeds and of establishing their fame for ever. And they used not to wish one another joy but for three things—the birth of a boy, the coming to light of a poet, and the foaling of a noble mare'.*

Pre-Islamic poetry was the natural expression of normal life so we might have expected that the new conditions and ideas introduced by Islam would create a revolution in the poetical literature of the following century. This was not so. Poets clung to the great models of the Heroic Age and even took credit for their skilful imitation of the antique odes. The early Mohammadan critics firmly stated that poetry in pre-Islamic times had reached a perfection which no modern bard could hope to emulate, and which only the lost ideals of chivalry could inspire.

Originality was condemned in advance and those who desired the approval of the powerful critics were obliged to waste their time and talents on elaborate reproductions of the ancient masterpieces.

Much poetry, before and after Islam, is vainglorious. The poet glorifies himself, his family and his tribe. No poet ever tires of proclaiming his valour and recounting his brilliant feats of arms. Poems are full of menaces and challenges, and obscenity is commonplace. Another constant theme is blood-revenge, with poems explaining the poet's courage and resolution, and contempt of death. They reveal extreme cruelty and ferocity and the poet, or his subject, is shown exulting over the corpses of men he has slain. The Arab hero is defiant and boastful and when there is little to lose he will ride off unashamed, but he will fight to the death for his women. In serious warfare the women often accompanied the tribe and were stationed behind the line of battle.

Some Arab stories reveal the ideal Arab hero, such as Shanfara of Azd and his comrade, Ta'abbata Sharran. Both were brigands, outlaws, swift runners, and excellent poets. As a child, Shanfara was captured by the Banu Salaman tribe and brought up among them. He did not learn his origin until he had grown up, when he vowed vengeance against his captors, and

* Ibn Rashiq in Suyuti's *Muzhir*, translated by Sir Charles Lyall in the Introduction to his *Ancient Arabian Poetry*, 1900.

returned to his own tribe. He swore that he would slay a hundred men of Salaman and he had slain ninety-eight when he was caught in an enemy ambush. In the struggle one of his hands was hewn off by a sword stroke, but taking the weapon in the other, he flung it in the face of the Salaman tribesman and killed him, thus making ninety-nine. Then he was overpowered and slain. As his skull lay bleaching on the ground, a man of his enemies passed by and kicked it; a splinter of bone entered his foot, the wound turned septic and he died, thus completing Shanfara's hundred.*

The Bedouin ideal of generosity and hospitality is personified in Hatim of Tayyi', of whom many anecdotes are told.

When Hatim's mother was pregnant she dreamed that she was asked, 'Which dost thou prefer?—a generous son called Hatim, or ten like those of other folk, lions in the hour of battle, brave lads and strong of limb?' and she answered, 'Hatim.' Now, when Hatim grew up he was wont to take out his food, and if he found any one to share it he would eat, otherwise he threw it away. His father, seeing that he wasted his food, gave him a slave-girl and a mare with her foal and sent him to herd the camels.

On reaching the pasture, Hatim began to search for his fellows, but none was in sight; then he came to the road, but found no one there. While he was thus engaged he descried a party of riders on the road and went to meet them. 'O youth,' said they, 'hast thou aught to entertain us withal?' He answered: 'Do ye ask me of entertainment when ye see the camels?' These riders were on their way to King Nu'man. Hatim slaughtered three camels for them, whereupon one man said: 'We desired no entertainment save milk, but if thou must needs charge thyself with something more, a single young she-camel would have sufficed us.' Hatim replied: 'That I know, but seeing different faces and diverse fashions I thought ye were not of the same country, and I

* *Ancient Arabian Poetry*, op. cit.

wished that each of you should mention what ye saw, on returning home.'

So they spoke verses in praise of him and celebrated his generosity, and Hatim said: 'I wished to bestow a kindness upon you, but your bounty is greater than mine. I swear to God that I will hamstring every camel in the herd unless ye come forward and divide them among yourselves.' The travellers did as he desired, and each man received ninety-nine camels; then they proceeded on their journey to Nu'man. When Hatim's father heard of this he came to him and asked, 'Where are the camels?' 'O my father,' replied Hatim, 'by means of them I have conferred on thee everlasting fame and honour that will cleave to thee like the ring of the ringdove, and men will always bear in mind some verse of poetry in which we are praised. This is thy recompense for the camels.'

On hearing these words his father said, 'Didst thou with my camels thus?'

'Yes.'

'By God I will never dwell with thee again!' So he went forth with his family, and Hatim was left alone with his slave-girl and his mare and the mare's foal.*

The poetry of Arabian women of the pre-Islamic period is distinctly masculine. Their songs are seldom of love, but often of death. Elegy or dirge was regarded as their special province. The poetess begins with a description of her grief, of the tears that she cannot quench. The dead man is described as a pattern of the two principal Arabian virtues, bravery and liberality, and the question is anxiously asked, 'Who will now make high resolves, overthrow the enemy, and in time of want feed the poor and entertain the stranger?' If the hero of the dirge died a violent death we find in addition a burning lust for revenge, a thirst for the slayer's blood, expressed with an intensity of feeling of which only women are capable.†

* From the *Kitabu 'l-Aghani* (The Book of Songs) of the thirteenth century.

† This information is taken from lengthy studies by the German scholar, Theodor Nöldeke.

The Arab poet, naturally enough, gave little attention to abstraction or pure thought. His mind focused on war, love, hunting, the desert and mountains, the foulness of enemies, the fame of friends. Equally understandably, poets became leaders of public opinion; their utterances took the place of political pamphlets and of party oratory.

For the modern historian their work is even more important for it is through the poets that we get the most detailed accounts of certain periods. The eleventh century's great Abu l'Ala, for instance, leaves no aspect of the age untouched, and presents a vivid picture of degeneracy and corruption, in which tyrannous rulers, venal judges, hypocritical and unscrupulous theologians, swindling astrologers, roving swarms of dervishes and godless Carmathians occupy a prominent place.

With such linguistic tradition it is hardly surprising that among Arabs words should become so important.

A modern Arab writer, Darwish al-Jundi,* has said:

'The Arabic language is the strongest foundation of Arab nationalism. It has drawn together the Arabs of various countries and has been the means of communication of both their mind and spirit since the emergence of Islam. The Arabic language is a record of Arab creativity, a symbol of their unity, and the expression of their intellectual and technical achievements. The Arabic language has displayed a tremendous vitality in its meticulous structure, its wide extension, and its flexibility, which has rendered it a fitting vehicle for the transmission of the arts and sciences. The imperialists were aware of the influence of the Arabic language drawing the Arabs together, in binding their past to their present, and in consolidating Arab nationalism. They fought it and tried to replace it with their own languages. They also attempted to develop colloquial and regional dialects, hoping thereby to stamp out classical Arabic, tear the links

* An Egyptian with Ph.D in Arabic literature. The passage appears in an essay in *Political and Social Thought in the Contemporary Middle East*, Praeger, 1968.

between Arabs, and weaken Arab sentiment, which is everywhere nourished by the language.'

This language is itself so extravagant in its dramatic and sweeping claims that it makes al-Jundi's point even more sharply than does his explanation.

The Arab's virtual obsession with oral functions can hardly escape notice; it strikes the observer in Arab reverence for language and oral arts as well as in the Arab attitude towards food. The richness of Arabic has an almost bewitching effect upon those for whom it is the native language. Gibb remarks, 'The medium in which the aesthetic feeling of the Arabs is mainly (though not exclusively) expressed is that of words and language—upon the Arab mind the impact of artistic speech is immediate; the words, passing through no filter or logic or reflection, which might weaken or deaden their effect, go straight to the head.'*

Oral communication assumes great importance in a society with high illiteracy, but the infatuation with 'artistic speech' and song extends to the literate Arab as well. Education and sophistication does not reduce the Arab's susceptibility to the charms of a good sermon, a political harangue, or the songs of popular male and female entertainers. Great value is put upon the ability to chant the Koran and to memorize it completely, and upon recitation or verbal dexterity in every conceivable form. For instance, oral testimony in Islamic law is superior to circumstantial evidence. An Arab political scientist, perhaps exaggerating out of dissatisfaction with Arab politics, has gone so far as to claim that aesthetic appreciation of the language has hindered its use as a means of conveying ideas clearly.

'Unless one is in full command of an idea,' he writes, 'and unless he has it precisely articulated in his head, he should not attempt to publish it in Arabic—for somewhere on the way he will eventually lose it and find himself, to his surprise, writing thoughts he never dreamed of.'†

* H. A. R. Gibb, *Modern Trends in Islam*, University of Chicago Press, 1947.
† Y. Salem, 'Form and Substance', an essay in *Middle East Forum*, July 1958.

Jacques Berque, French student of Arab and Moslem affairs, has remarked that the Oriental prefers words to things and speech to action because he has not mastered the world of things. To the Westerner, Nature rules but can be mastered if understood; to the Oriental, Nature simply rules.*

Eli Shouby has claimed that the difference between the 'ideal' and 'real' language create deep repercussions in the Arab personality structure. He sees literary Arabic as the 'ideal self of the Arabs' while colloquial Arabic is 'the monopoly of the practical functions of the real self'.†

It is sometimes claimed that the Arabic language is an idiom more 'associative' in its structure than 'logical and analytical' and attempts have been made to draw from this theory the conclusion that the language itself is not suited to logical thinking. This is an over-simplification, yet there is some truth in the observation, especially in relation to everyday spoken language, that is the dialects in which Arabs of all countries verbally express themselves while using the classical language as a written language. The dialects are full of allusions and approximations; slightly varying expressions are repeated twice or three times to make them clearly understood and are accompanied by the very commonly used *'ya'ani'*, or 'that means'.

Poetry is today, as it was thirteen hundred years ago, a part of everyday living. People improvise it by way of a pastime or quote it as a means of communication. Versification appeals even to the illiterate, who usually know a certain number of famous verses and recite them at every opportunity.

Arabic's wealth of synonyms provides for unrivalled possibilities in figurative speech. It has many innuendoes, tropes and figures of speech. In addition, it possesses many stylistic and grammatical peculiarities. With its phonetic beauty, richness of synonyms, figurative speech, rhythm and majesty, the Arabic

---

* Jacques Berque, 'Leçon inaugurale', Collège de France, Paris, 1956.
† Eli Shouby, 'The Influence of the Arabic Language on Psychology of the Arabs', *Middle East Journal*, Summer 1951.

language arouses the passion of the people. Arabs love their language as vividly today as they ever did. Enjoying its floweriness and power, they speak it with distinction and precision and play with its characteristic eloquence. Oratory and extemporaneous speech occupy an important place among the Arabs, who have a talent of speech, an abundant verbal facility, and skill in expressing one single idea under multiple forms.

But thoughts expressed in Arabic are generally vague and hard to pin down. Writing that deals with simple or familiar questions creates no difficulties; but the more novel or abstract the content, the more difficult it is to understand Arabic with accuracy. While it is possible to understand an ordinary Arabic sentence as a whole, to understand it in a manner that fits all the details into a clear and well-integrated picture is not always easy. However, if the Arab understands the general meaning or significance of a sentence or a paragraph, with all its effective colouring and intuitive revelations, he will think that he understands it perfectly and accurately.*

The rapid influx of Western culture into the Arab world forced writers into the use of old words for the explanation of new ideas. Furthermore, the same word has different connotations when used by different persons. Yet the main cause for Arabic vagueness of thought is in the fact that modern literary Arabic is an amalgam of diffuse, undifferentiated and rigid units and structures. For instance, there is a strict insistence on the rigid grammatical and formal aspects of the language although some of these forms are obsolete. For a writer to be successful, it does not matter if he makes his sentences only diffusely comprehensible, provided he sticks to the correct grammatical and idiomatic aspects of the language. He does not seem to be much concerned about making his meaning clear-cut and unequivocal.†

The impact of words and forms counts more than the transmission of ideas. 'Instead of manipulating the linguistic tools

---

* Eli Shouby, op. cit.   † Ibid.

to make them convey his thoughts and ideas in an appropriate manner, he forces his thoughts to accommodate themselves to the readymade linguistic structure which he borrows from general rule.'*

Arabic literature and language over-emphasize the significance of words as such and pay less attention to their meaning. An aspect of this situation is the Arab's delight in 'playing with words'. There are numerous repetitions of the same ideas in different words. Various words are used for the same meaning. There are also abrupt transitions. The tendency to fit the thought to the word, or to the combination of words, rather than the word to the thought is a result of the psychological replacement of thoughts by words, which become the substitutes for thoughts and not their representatives.

The writer engages in the task of surprising his readers or listeners with his description. He does not care for the incident, facts, or ideas he is trying to portray, and is swayed by the display of his literary skill, wit and erudition. His effect is shown in his virtuosity. 'The author outweighs the word, and effect relegates truth to the background.'†

The range of intellectual activity considered subject to the laws of literary style has constantly widened and elegance of presentation became obligatory. Illustrations culled from poems, anecdotes, and parables were discovered as effective means to please the public; frequent switches from one subject to another would keep fatigue from the reader. Effortless instruction, amusing edification, and informative witticism were eagerly applauded. The result was the philosophical causerie, a gossipy and clever historiography, the encyclopaedia, or simply a collection of miscellaneous and unintegrated information interspersed with rhymes and stories—all these presented in a glamorous garb of verbal splendour. Style came to be cultivated for its own sake, wit degenerated into punning,

* Eli Shouby, op. cit.
† G. E. von Grunebaum, 'Islam: A Study in Cultural Orientation', an essay, London, 1962.

and the substance of what the author had set out to convey almost evaporated into fireworks of rhetoric.*

This over-emphasis of the value of words and the beauty of style is further strengthened by the pleasure derived from the sound of words and the rhythm and harmony produced by their combinations. The phonetic beauty of the Arabic language and the musicality of its words invite emotional response and weaken the faculty of reasoning.

The Arab's lingering over details is well represented in modern poetry. Here he renders each point with poignancy, but usually lets escape the totality of the person or object he is describing. The same thing is true of the writer who excels in the observation of details, 'but, for the most part, he is unable or perhaps unwilling, to synthesize his impressions'. These he strings on to one another with little regard to the unity of the personality he depicts or of the literary composition in which he is engaged.†

Because of overstressing of details, without giving an organized whole, to convey meaning in ordinary conversation it is necessary to repeat oneself several times through different words. Thus, a great deal is lost by translating a Western language if there is no assertion or exaggeration. This need for repetition is seen when a guest is invited to eat. Etiquette requires that he refuse several times before he finally accepts, thus a simple refusal is never taken at its face value, which naturally leads to misunderstandings with a person from the Western world. Again, in the Middle East, bargaining in selling and buying, because of the linguistic opportunities, becomes almost an art.

This is more than can be said of education. The Arab method of teaching and learning is based, just as in the middle ages, on learning by rote. For many centuries no books were available and the Arab world was without a printing press until 1821. A teacher took a group of pupils under the shade of a tree and

* G. E. von Grunebaum, op. cit.
† Ibid.

presented them with information from his head which he saw was instilled into *their* heads by repetition.

Students can be seen today memorizing their textbooks, page by page and, because Arab students usually have an excellent memory, the method is pernicious. They ask each other: 'What appears on page 43?' And they answer by reciting the text beginning with the first word on that page, even if it forms part of a sentence begun on the previous page. 'Knowledge' consists very often of literally knowing the words of a text and not of understanding its meaning. It is profoundly difficult to change these methods of teaching. The learning by heart and repetition always creep in. Such a system permits only superficial examinations of knowledge and this increases the tendency. The teacher himself often knows nothing more than the business of learning by heart. He himself went to a school where the textbooks used to be recited in chorus until the 'gifted' pupils—those endowed with a good memory—could declaim them by heart. During the examinations, these texts are examined. A professor at an Arab university who refuses to identify the textbook and tell the students the page numbers which will be used in the examination, or one who poses a question that cannot be answered with a phrase learnt by heart from a book or solved through the use of a formula found in a book, will face a rebellion from students, their parents, even from the university authorities. They will force him to give in or to resign.

All this fosters the belief in words and thinking in terms of words. 'Truths' are being 'learnt' by heart; repetition replaces comprehension. The posing of questions as to the meaning of a word, of a sentence, of a theory, of an assertion is blocked. This learned-by-heart aspect of many political 'opinions', and the explanation of processes which often consist of no more than loosely piled up catchwords, can frequently be perceived. There is the deliberation of recitation in the learned tone, and a question as to what is *meant* provokes the same recitation in a louder voice and, finally, the same again in a more angry and irritated tone. The question 'What do you understand by "colonialism"?' will at most receive the answer, '"Exploitation" of a weak nation by a militarily superior nation.'

'What is to be understood by exploitation? How can it be demonstrated?'

'It consists of taking away the riches of the poor countries and using them for the enrichment of the rich nations.'

How it works and of what it actually consists can only rarely be asked. Anger over constant questioning about 'truths', that everybody after all knows, will, almost as a rule, put an end to the game.

After such a conversation one has the feeling that the other party is content with recording the emotional content, that 'colonialism' is something bad under which we suffer and against which we must fight; it comes from the 'West' and has to do with the avarice of the Europeans and Americans.

An Arab word corresponding to a European concept must often be coined anew. Arabic does not tolerate foreign words, the way Turkish or Persian absorb them without difficulty. Instead, it makes use of the wealth of its word roots and all their possible modifications in order to coin new expressions. The expressions are simply defined as corresponding to one or another French or English word. Because such coinings bear a similarity to Arabic, sound like other Arabic words and appear to be so reliable, there is still less questioning of their meaning than would be the case with foreign words, which immediately display their newness and strangeness by their linguistic form. They are taken over in an intercourse of language and thought, often without an examination as to their content.

It is difficult for an outsider to imagine the degree in which modern newspaper Arabic contains such 'coined' concepts, which are nothing but Arab garments for English or French concepts, not always familiar to the reader, or which are imitations in Arabic of superfluous but convenient English or French phraseology. This can be tested by asking an educated Arab about the meaning of various abstract words that appear in every political speech and newspaper article. He will cite as an 'explanation' the English or French expression of which the Arabic is an imitation. What about someone who does not understand English or French? Their comprehension of concepts which are repeated every day, such as socialism, communism, nationalism, reaction, progressivism, freedom, state, fatherland, nation and many others, must frequently remain imprecise and limited, without a clear understanding of their meaning.

None of this is meant to imply that Arabs are obtuse; their intellects have been obstructed by a system which gives no credit for original thought and has no tradition of research. As von Grunebaum has pertinently observed, 'The results of Western research are more easily transferable than its methods and the Western research mentality, one of the most singular characteristics of our culture, can only very gradually be instilled into the thoughts and the feelings of the impatient young nationalists of the Near East.'*

The first time I visited an Arab school—in a refugee camp in South Lebanon—I was invited to listen to some lessons, which as it happened, were on English Literature. The teacher's technique was, of course, one of group interrogation with conditioned responses. After each question the entire class of about forty boys would shout their answer.

Teacher: From what part of England did William Wordsworth come?

Boys: William Wordsworth came from the Lake District!

Teacher: What did William Wordsworth write about?

Boys: William Wordsworth wrote about nature!

Teacher: Which kind of people did William Wordsworth like most of all?

Boys: William Wordsworth liked the common people most of all!

In my innocence—at that time—I asked if I might talk to

* G. E. von Grunebaum, op cit.

the boys and ask some questions. Not until later did I realize the agony I caused some boys by asking them questions they could not answer. They were shamed in front of their fellows. They were also bewildered: they had been told I was an 'expert' on English Literature, so why was I asking them questions? It was my business to be giving information, not seeking it.

The old order is being challenged, but not very successfully because, by tradition, tradition cannot be criticized. The ideal —I speak in the abstract, not as a Western writer—will be reached when Arab education can be based on stimulating discussion between teacher and students and on reason rather than recitation. With so many Arab students gaining degrees in Western universities and taking back to their homelands the revolutionary concept that education is as much a matter of learning as it is of teaching, there is some hope that language and literature will become more constructive.

Some Arabs have been critical of Arabic language and literature and education, though to be so takes much courage. In 1926 the great Egyptian novelist and literary historian, Taha Husayn, published an analysis of pre-Islamic poetry which caused such a scandal that it was withdrawn. Husayn, applying modern critical scholarship to the ancient poetry of Arabia, doubted whether it had in fact been written before Islam. This suggested a critical method which, if applied to the texts of religion, might cast doubts on their authenticity, and it struck at the roots of the traditional structure of Arabic learning by which the faith was supported. Opposition to Husayn was orally and physically violent.

As much courage is needed for an Arab woman to be critical, especially of men. The Palestinian poetess, Fadwa Touqan, invited abuse and threats with a poem published in the East Jerusalem Arab-language daily newspaper, *Al-Quds.**

* June 5, 1972. The English translation was published in *New Middle East*, April 1973.

O my people! Till where and when?
That you might charge and conquer, we would embrace and
   spread the pillows;
Or you might retreat; then we would part, forever without
   love!
Still in the anaesthesia chambers we slumber;
And years go by, year after year after year.
The earth rumbles beneath our feet,
And the ceiling is falling heaps of rubble, upon us;
And in falsehood we are submerged,
From the tops of our heads to our toes.
O my people! till where and when?
Oh Vietnam, we call you in pain.
Oh! If only one million warriors from among your heroes,
   were blown by an easterly wind
Upon the Arabian Desert;
Pillows would be spread,
And one million Kahtani [Palestinian] child-bearing women
Would be bestowed upon thee!

Forgiveness! Forgiveness O men of the household,
For piercing indeed is this desire.
But the oil-jug anecdote has exhausted all our patience,
For are lost all substances, all original things,
And you left us nothing to behold,
But the crackling voice.
And we are weary, O my beloved,
Of sprinkling sugar upon Death!

Palestinian men were intensely ashamed by the poem—and
more by imputations against their courage than by the offer
of their women to mate with Vietnamese warriors.

Betrayal is a theme of Miss Touqan's poem and this and
violence are frequently found in modern Arab novels. Some
Arabic books would be untranslatable because of the blood-
lust which permeates them. Details about smashing the human
body reach a hideous obscenity—and this in books which

claim to be novels rather than slick and racy yarns. The Arab writer also has great difficulty in his treatment of sex. Western novels show that it is possible for women to have jobs and yet lead a sex life; the idea is implicit and so natural that no writer questions it. But even among the best Arab novelists, women are merely sex objects. Arab male novelists include female characters for no other purpose than to create sex situations. No deliberate degradation is intended; the writers have the authority of the Prophet that women are inferior, so the novelists are treating them normally.

This necessarily brief analysis of Arabic language and literature emphasizes the richness of Arabic but it would be wrong to think that Arabs never talk in commonplaces. Much conversation is as inconsequential as it is flowery but it is rare for an Arab mind to admit this.

Kamel Nasser, senior spokesman for the Palestine Liberation Organisation in Beirut before his death in an Israeli raid on terrorist bases in April 1973, complained to me that he always had difficulty in framing Press releases after P.L.O. meetings. 'I never know quite how to write a report,' he said. 'If I write down everything that is said at a meeting I would have enough material for a book. If I report the essence of a meeting I mostly find that the whole thing had been a waste of time. So I go to Arafat and say, "What do you want me to tell the Press?" He replies, "Tell them the truth." I have to tell him that this particular case does not concern truth but the P.L.O.'s official attitude to King Hussein.

' "Then tell the Press the truth about Hussein," Arafat says. "You know what to say about Hussein—he is an imperialist and a murderer. He is the pariah of the Arab world. He takes bribes and lives off American and British money." '

Nasser, a likeable but nervy man, put his hands to his head in despair. 'Do you know, Arafat has never said either "Yes" or "No" to me when I ask him a direct question. You would think he could do that much for his Press officer!'

I sympathized with him. 'Do you like Arafat?' I asked.

And Nasser replied, 'It's not a matter of liking or disliking . . . '

In my three long talks with him he, too, never once said 'Yes' or 'No'.

Arabic conversation is full of 'secrets'. Behavioural experiments are fairly rare in Arab societies but those that have been conducted are interesting. A large number of Egyptian children aged eight to eleven years were told: 'Mohammad takes Ali behind a shed and whispers to him. *What* does he whisper?' Such experiments are commonplace in Western societies and the usual 'secret' produced by children is some childish sexual indiscretion or some mischievous plot. In the Egyptian experiment nearly ninety per cent of the children gave, in essence, this response: 'Mohammad whispers to Ali, "You know that Mustapha pretends to be your friend? In fact, he is betraying you. But I am your friend." '

For the Arab there is yet another form of communication —by gestures. For Arabs of all social levels, gestures are an indispensable part of any conversation. To tie an Arab's hands while he is speaking is tantamount to tying his tongue. Robert Barakat, an anthropologist at Newfoundland's Memorial University, recently gathered a dictionary of gestures from throughout the Arab world and was able to give specific definitions to no fewer than 247.

Although the majority of the gestures are obscene, many serve to convey respectable and useful information. If, for instance, a man in Saudi Arabia kisses the top of another man's head, it is a sign of apology. In Jordan and three other Arab countries, to flick the right thumbnail against the front teeth means the gesturer has no money or only a little. Bedouin touch their noses three times to show friendship. In Libya, it is customary for men to twist the tips of their forefingers into their cheeks when speaking to beautiful women.

Many of the gestures are tacit tools of flirtation. Northern

Syrians blow smoke in a woman's face to show that they desire her. In Lebanon, the same message is conveyed by punching the left palm with a closed right fist.

All Arabs, according to Barakat, share a certain basic vocabulary of body language. They stand close together and frequently touch each other in a conversation, and they look each other in the eye constantly, instead of letting their gaze drift to the side as most Westerners do. Gesturing is done with the right hand, not the 'unclean' left.

While Arabs also employ some Western gestures—they tease one another by sticking out their tongues—a few crucial gestures mean diametrically opposite things in the two cultures. When Arabs shake their heads from side to side, they are saying yes instead of no. Moreover, when Arabs mean no, they move the head upward (and click with the tongue), seeming to Western eyes, to nod assent. Apparently most foreigners find it easy to switch to the Arab system. Barakat relates the story of an English teacher in the Middle East whose wife had remained behind in England. When one of his Arab students left for a trip to England, the teacher suggested that the young man look up his wife while he was there. The student did, and had an affair with the lonely woman. On returning home for a visit the Englishman asked his wife if the Arab had paid a call. Reacting guiltily, the wife denied having met the student—by snapping her head upward and clicking her tongue.

Arabic might be rich in gestures, but the limitation of language was recognized by Gamal Abdel Nasser. One of the principal leaders of the coup which overthrew King Farouk in 1952, Nasser was perturbed on the evening of the coup to find an associate agitated and emotional. Nasser told the man, in English, 'Tonight there is no room for sentiment; we must be ready for the unexpected.'

Asked why he had spoken in English, the future President of Egypt replied that Arabic was not a suitable language in which to express the need for calm. Nasser demonstrated how Arabic provides flexibility. King Hussein was at one time a 'prostitute', but when he was more inclined to do what Nasser wanted he became a 'great brother'. Again Nasser labelled the Ba'ath regime in Syria as 'progressive, socialist and revolutionary' —all complimentary terms. But in a statement of August 12, 1963, the Syrian leaders were 'fascist', 'Nazi' and 'dictatorial'.

I can best illustrate the elasticity of Arabic by a story whose authenticity I can vouch for. At the time of the Arab–Israeli Six-Day War in June 1967 an Israeli and an Egyptian professor were colleagues, and good friends, at an American university. The Arab defeat was so rapid and shaming that the Egyptian disappeared from the Faculty Common Room and was not seen for more than two weeks. The Israeli wondered how best to greet his friend when he at last reappeared. But the initiative was taken by the Egyptian who turned up in the Common Room one lunchtime and came across the floor with his arms outstretched for embrace and his face broad with a smile. His first words were declaimed vigorously: 'Ah, my friend—what a magnificent defeat we achieved!'

We are left, then, with some profoundly significant conclusions which anybody dealing with Arabs must understand. They are worth stressing:

To the Arab there may be several truths about the one situation, depending on the type of language he is using.

A linguistic truth over-rides a perceptual one; that is, what language can be made to say about a situation has more validity than what the eyes or reason might say.

Language is not used to reason, but to persuade.

Literature exists to persuade (e.g. the Koran) and to delight; it is not designed to stimulate the intellect but to incite the senses.

The Arab means what he says at the moment he is saying it. He is neither a vicious nor, usually, a calculating liar but a natural one.

Meanings are not constant from one person to another.

The value of words is often assessed by quantity.

Words can justify or rationalize anything.

The greater the rhetoric, the lesser the substance.

When the Arab speaks in slogans he is regurgitating propaganda.

Language creates violence, justifies it and excuses it.

We must be patient with the Arab in discussion; he is intellectually incapable of coming directly to the point.

5 *The Shame Society*

'With the sword will I wash my shame away.
Let God's doom bring on me what it may!'
Abu Tamman, ninth-century poet, in Hamasa.

'We are a people that never forgets if it has been injured, but the injury to us increases our determination and stubbornness.' President Nasser, March 3, 1955.

'To die, to be ignorant, to be incapable, to do under compulsion, deafness, blindness and to be incapable of saying, are all defects. They are things to be ashamed of.' Halid-e Bagdadee, *Belief and Islam*, Istanbul, 1973.

Arab society is a shame society, says Sania Hamady. Such an unequivocal statement by an Arab scholar needs amplification for it would be natural enough to think, from what follows in this chapter, that I am dealing with a type of behaviour that could only be described as aberrant. From the Arab viewpoint it is normative; it is aberrant only to the Western mind. A culture-bound approach blinds one to the problem and it is the responsibility of Westerners to perceive—and resolve—it. Arabs are accustomed to masking motives and are so subjective that they have no perspective about shame, honour and revenge.

As a result of tribal values, Arab society demands a high degree of conformity which in turn confers a strong authoritarian tone. Conformity in itself brings honour and social prestige and a secure place in society; while the individual conforms his in-group members and associates are bound to help his interests and they will defend him unquestioningly against 'outsiders'.

Failure to conform is damning and leads to a degree of shame that is difficult for a Western Christian or a Jew to conceive. Also, in Arab attitudes shame has a further dimension; it not only means commission of some act against the accepted system of values but the discovery by outsiders that the act has been committed.

Hamady puts it this way: 'He who has done a shameful deed must conceal it, for revealing one disgrace is to commit another disgrace.' A proverb is more succinct: 'A concealed sin is two-thirds forgiven.' And the usual Arab reply to the courtesy inquiry of 'How are things?' is most revealing of all. A man will say '*Mastur al-hal*' which means idiomatically 'We're all right.' Literally the meaning is 'The condition is covered.' Shame must be avoided; if it strikes, then it must be hidden; if it is exposed, then it must be avenged. At all costs, honour must be restored.

The fear of shame among Arabs is so powerful because the identification between the individual and the group is far closer than in the West; the shamed individual could lose his influence and power and through him the group will similarly suffer, perhaps to the point of destruction.

From top to bottom Arab society is permeated by a system of rival relationships. It is fed by the simple fact that in the Arab value system a major attribute of prestige is the ability to dominate others. In the constant struggle to dominate and to resist domination the rivals of a given individual or group quickly seize on any 'shame' to destroy its influence. This is achieved as effectively by isolating the 'target' as by physically destroying it. Arabs fear isolation because the individual or group can function effectively only when he or it is identified with a group or a larger body that can offer protection.

Shame is eliminated by revenge, and this is sanctioned by Islam (Koran, sura xi, 173): 'Believers, retaliation is decreed for you in bloodshed.' It may also be eliminated by payment by kinsmen of the author of the crime or by the public treasury. In the case of a killing the price of the blood will be sent to the family of the victim.

The need for revenge is as strong today as ever and is illustrated by the proliferation of vengeance-related feuds and murders. In Egypt in 1972 in 1,120 cases of murder where the criminal was caught (another 4,000 were not solved) it was found that 25 per cent of the murders were based on the urge to 'wipe out shame', 30 per cent on a desire to satisfy 'wrongs' and another 30 per cent on blood-revenge.

The depth of emotion involved in Arab feelings is clearly shown in the utterance of the Shi-ite Chief Mujtahid of Iraq in August 1938. In declaring a jihad for Palestine (a decade before the creation of Israel) he said that fighting would be the duty of everybody and that if the Arabs lost they would suffer 'humiliation, death and eternal shame'.

When this degree of feeling is reached peace is a secondary consideration, and this leads to the impression that in the Arab context peace is merely the temporary absence of conflict. In Arab tribal society, where Arab values originated, strife was the normal state of affairs because raiding was one of the two main supports of the economy. In Islam the ideal of permanent peace was restricted to the community of Islam and to those non-Moslems who accepted the position of protected persons and paid tribute to Islam. With regard to non-Moslem states, Islam instituted jihad as the accepted relationship and made no provision for peace with them as sovereign and independent entities. Only a truce was permissible, and that was not to last for more than ten years.

Arabs consider time to be of little account in the quest for vengeance, which to them is an integral part of what they conceive of as 'justice'. Some vendettas among Arabs have lasted for centuries.

Arab writings and lectures are full of frustration and shame. Abdul Aziz Said, a professor of political philosophy in the United States, told a conference* about his student days at the end of World War II and just after.

* The annual conference of the American Academic Association for Peace in the Middle East, 1971.

'I remember our lengthy meetings on the street corners of Damascus, Beirut and Cairo, our heated debates in coffee shops and our constant arguments over Arab unity and socialism. In the meantime, Israel defeated the Arabs [1948]. The Arab world was outraged. We demonstrated [in Syria] for the restoration of Arab honour. Colonel Husni al-Zaim answered our prayers with a military coup and a promise of Utopia. President al-Kuwatli, founding father of Syria, was declared a traitor. No sooner did we learn to dance to Colonel Zaim's baton than he was executed for treason. We cheered our new messiah, Colonel Sami al-Hinnawi. But he too did not last. We demonstrated again. Arab streets are filled with the debris of frustrated dreams and abandoned schemes, as each new prophet attacks his predecessor with gay abandon.'

President Nasser was 'ashamed' as early in his career as 1942. At that time Hitler* was tremendously popular with the Arabs and Egypt had a pro-Nazi Prime Minister and Chief of Staff, both of whom were removed by the British. Nasser and other young officers of the Egyptian Army were distressed and Nasser wrote to a friend, 'I am ashamed that our army has not reacted against this attack but I am glad that our officers, who until now think only of amusing themselves, at last begin to speak of revenge.'†

Fortunately, for themselves and for others, Arabs often find enough solace in speaking about revenge rather than seeking it. It is true there are corpses enough to show that revenge is achieved but if words were bullets there would be millions more dead.

On the personal, family level shame often results in tragedy. It is a matter of honour for the man of the family to kill a woman who has 'sinned'. In an incident known to me a family poisoned a daughter because her husband found she was not a virgin on marriage.

* 'The greatest contemporary Arab hero is Adolf Hitler.' John Gunther, *Inside Asia*, Harper & Bros, New York, 1939.
† Robert St John, *The Boss*, McGraw-Hill, 1960.

In Cairo in April 1974 a man in his late twenties killed his mother, a widow, because she had been seeing another man. As he explained, this was 'shame on my father's memory'. Since he had been in custody four days before the court hearing, the murderer was released without further punishment.

In another case, a man wrote to the 'Personal Problems' column of a Cairo newspaper to say that a few months earlier he had killed his wife's lover and had been gaoled. His wife and child had visited him during his six months' gaol term and he now wanted the editor to tell him if he was right in his decision to return to his wife and live with her. The editor, a woman, brushed this question aside, and asked one of her own. 'Why did you kill the man and not your wife?'*

An American ethnographer, Richard T. Antoun, produced an interesting case study of shame and its results while researching in the east Jordanian village of Kufr al-Ma in the 1960s. The tragedy began when police picked up three young men in a taxi with the daughter of a prominent member of a local family, a man who had once served as mayor of Kufr al-Ma. The girl's father was also related to the leading notable of the area, formerly a member of the Jordanian Senate. His family and economic ties to Kufr al-Ma village were of long standing. The Pasha, as he was called in recognition of his position, had similar ties in several other villages.

The three young men found with the Pasha's kinswoman had intended to take her to a resort in the Jordan Valley where they had once before plied her with liquor and then had sexual relations with her. Two of the young men were cousins and members of the Zaydan clan and lived in Deir Abu Said where the father of one had a successful grocery shop. The people of the Zaydan were regarded with disfavour by many of the villagers in Kufr al-Ma because they had occupied Kufr al-Ma in the nineteenth century, although later driven out. According to the villagers, they had been involved in other cases

* In Egypt a man who kills his wife's lover is sentenced to a maximum of ten years' gaol; the maximum penalty for killing a wife is four years.

of immorality that had been shamefully settled through bribery.

One of the young men had become familiar with the girl at her father's farm in the Jordan Valley, a farm which he had often ploughed with his tractor. The other had been seen loitering near the girl's house in Kufr al-Ma. She kept house for her brother who was at school in the next town while the rest of the family lived in the Jordan Valley. The loiterer had been liaising between the girl and his cousin, arranging the time and place of rendezvous.

The three men were gaoled and the girl was released into her father's custody. It was quite clear that she had not objected; she gave no cries of alarm and did not inform any member of her family of molestation.

For several weeks there were informal negotiations for a money settlement and a quashing of the case. The four families who comprised the Zaydan tribe continued living in Deir Abu Said, assuming that some settlement could be reached, but they proposed neither elopement nor marriage for the girl and any one of her paramours, a customary solution that might have saved her life. The testimony of the culprits was now public knowledge; they frequently confessed to their actions in detail. This increased the pressure on the girl's father to take action.

A member of the Zaydan approached a prominent elder of the other tribe to ask about the possibility of 'sanctuary' under the protection of another clan who would look after the property of the offenders and their relatives and make arrangements for an eventual peacemaking. Under such an agreement the offenders and their immediate relatives are banished from the area and so their property is at risk. Other more distant relatives must also seek the protection of 'sanctuary' even though they remain in their houses and on their lands, for their property is also open to theft and damage by the victim's group.

The Pasha, hearing of this approach, called in the leading men of the surrounding villages and urged them, for his honour, to refuse sanctuary. They obeyed him.

The girl's father and the Pasha took her to the town of Irbid for medical examination. She was no longer a virgin. (The autopsy after her death discovered her to be three months' pregnant.) The father returned with his daughter to his home in the Jordan Valley and early next day, on the morning of the great Moslem 'Festival of Sacrifice', he took her to Deir Abu Said. On the doorstep of the guardian of the guilty young men —father of one and uncle of the other—he stabbed her with his dagger. The killing on the doorstep was to show the guardian that he was responsible for the shame brought upon the girl, the loss of her kinsman's honour, and her death.

News of the girl's death reached Kufr al-Ma as the men of the village left the mosque after the Festival prayers. They set out in a body for Deir Abu Said. The girl's father had surrendered himself after the murder, so the mob besieged the police station and demanded to see him. When he appeared they cheered him. Dozens of relations of the young men, including those linked only through the paternal great-great-grandfather, had to leave the area; other even more distant relations paid a bribe known as 'the sleeping camel' to be allowed to remain. The killer father was released unpunished but later one of the young men was unaccountably murdered—by his father, it was assumed. Honour had been satisfied but it will take decades for the shame to be fully expunged.

One of the most recent incidents of this type occurred among Israeli Arabs. Abdullah Zeidan, of Yama, a village near Tulkarm, found out that his unmarried daughter, Husniya, was not a virgin. Aided and abetted by his son, Zeidan beat the girl to death with a pick. In July 1974 the District Court sentenced both men to life imprisonment. When they heard the sentence the women of the family present in court started wailing and banging their heads against the walls.

A Syrian scholar, Kazem Daghestani, tells of an Arab husband who caught his wife in bed with another man. He drew a gun and pointed it at the couple while addressing the man. 'I could kill you with one shot but I will let you go if you swear to keep secret the relationship you have had with my wife. If you ever talk about it I will kill you.' The man took that oath and left and the husband divorced his wife without divulging the cause. He was not concerned about the loss of his wife or her punishment but about his reputation. Public shaming, and not the nature of the deed itself or the individual's feelings, had determined his action.

Shame is revealed in other, less direct ways. The Egyptian novelist, Taha Husayn, describes, in an autobiographical story, an incident about a blind boy. He gives more attention to the boy's shame and embarrassment at his clumsiness while eating than to his inadequacy, for example, in running and playing with other children. He describes how the blind boy tried one day to eat a morsel of food with two hands instead of one 'as was customary'. His brothers laughed at him and his parents were critical. This incident of failure in eating etiquette deeply affected the boy; it 'curbed his curiosity, and filled his heart with a shyness which lingers even yet'. It is hard to imagine such a situation in a comparable Western home.

Social pressure in Arab society is tremendous. Public opinion is the main force that judges, praises or condemns the behaviour of the individual; it leaves him little choice for directing his own conduct. Since the internal freedom he enjoys is very slight, he is constantly watching for the opinions of his community. One of the basic problems of life in Arab society is the fear of each other's opinion. The object of fear is personified in society. As it curbs his actions, threatens him with constant shame, and often misjudges his acts, the Arab feels society to be his worst enemy. Rarely does he receive credit for his good deeds, but if he errs, the whip of society is always ready to lash.

As Hamady stresses, Arab morality depends on the pressure of an audience. *Hushûma*, another term that stands for shame, timidity, reserve, and control, strips him of spontaneity and liberty of action. Worry about external dignity is his continual concern. Even when he has a choice his standard is not whether his action would fulfil a function, answer a need, be expedient or convenient, but whether he would be ashamed if people knew about it. 'What would people say?' is the main criterion for his choice.

The change in the behaviour of an Arab once he has left the circle where he is known has startled observers. Arabs who have any status despise menial and manual work and members of good families would rather starve than be shamed by living by a humble occupation. But these people often go abroad and take up menial work, such as waiting at table, without feeling any loss of face. Women who usually live in segregation take off their veil and mix with men when in the company of foreigners. There is yet another escape-clause proverb for such occasions: 'Where you are not known do whatever you like.' This accounts for the large numbers of wealthy Arabs who visit Paris, London, New York and Rome for indulgence in Western vice.

Because social pressure in his home environment is constant the individual's conscience soon weakens. Hamady's observation that 'Lying is a widespread habit among the Arabs [who] have a low idea of the truth' is merely an echo of the medieval Moslem theologian al-Ghazali.

'Know that a lie is not wrong in itself, but only because of the evil conclusions to which it leads the hearer, making him believe something that is not really the case. Ignorance sometimes is an advantage, and if a lie causes this kind of ignorance it may be allowed. It is sometimes a duty to lie . . . if lying and truth both lead to a good result, you must tell the truth, for a lie is forbidden in this case. If a lie is the only way to reach a good result, it is allowable. A lie is lawful when it is the only path to duty. . . . We must lie when truth leads to unpleasant results, but tell the truth when it leads to good results.'

The Arab has no scruples about lying if by it he obtains his objective. His conscience possesses 'an interesting elasticity'.*

* Sania Hamady, op. cit.

To be frank does not pay among people who admire the clever and despise the meek. This particular trait may have been forced on the Arab because he has always been ruled by external or internal colonizers. The average Arab was forced to learn to conceal his hatred of and resentment towards his rulers; he had to feign submission in order to wrest from them what little he could.

Reputation is especially important and in this connection Arabs know the honour of the family as "*'ird*", a word with many variations. For instance, *'ird* is a matter of reputation even more than of fact. What other people think becomes as important as what takes place. An advance from a man, even if the woman is blameless, dishonours the family if the advance is observed by or becomes known to others. Hence, boasting of one's conquests endangers the social fabric, since it obliges the family of the woman to punish her and oneself. An offence against *'ird* —violence or adultery—may receive only a light penalty, unless it is publicly recognized and acknowledged. Like many other transgressions of the norms, the offences against *'ird* become very serious when public notice is taken of them.

'Ird appears in another sense in an interview with a Palestinian head of family, who was asked to describe his experience in leaving his village home in the June War of 1967.* In his answer he made the statement '*shirridna bi-'irdna*'—'We ran away with our honour intact.' His usage is interesting for two reasons. In the first place, the action to which he refers involved both components of *'ird*: the honour of the women and the response to physical challenge. By the standards of *'ird*, he had responded satisfactorily to the first component, saving the honour of his women, but failed to respond to the second, the challenge of the occupying army. To him, the first component justified his action. It took precedence over the second: honour of the women outweighed his honour as a fighter. This ranking of values is striking.

---

* P. Dodd and H. Barakat, *River Without Bridges: A Study of the Exodus of the 1967 Palestinian Refugees*, Beirut, 1969.

A second point is the use of the plural: 'We ran with our honour.' This suggests that the honour in question is a collective possession, something that belongs to more than one individual. This is certainly the feeling I have when speaking with Arabs.

The possibility of failure in any way fills the Arab with dread, for this, too, leads to shame. Naturally, such fear deters him from accepting responsibility. I referred earlier to an Egyptian Air Force officer who told me that Egyptian politicians had made a great mistake in buying Russian-built MIG aircraft —'It is too much responsibility to expect us to fly these planes,' he said more than once. It became clear that his fear of failure, and its attendant shame, was pathological.

At every opportunity the Arab underlines his belief that he has not failed, a habit that can be found in writings where no mention of either success or failure is necessary. Hasan al-Banna in a long essay on Islam, Modernism and Socialism,* using an aside to illustrate a point, expresses himself this way: 'In a whimsical moment, I happened to say to my audience at a meeting—*which, thanks to God, was a complete success* [my italics]—that this Islamic prayer which we perform five times a day is nothing but a daily training in practical social organization uniting the features of the Communist regime with those of the dictatorial and democratic regimes. . . .'

If, despite all efforts to succeed, failure becomes imminent the Arab must find somebody to blame—and because of his dependence this is not usually difficult. But because of his exalted position, President Nasser faced a dilemma when it became evident that the Arabs had lost their war against the Israelis in June 1967. Having nobody within Egypt on whom he could focus blame and expect it to stick, he telephoned King Hussein to discuss the 'cover story' to explain the defeat. They would blame American and perhaps British military intervention.

As Dr Hamady stresses, 'The Arabs usually look for external

* *Political and Social Thought in the Contemporary Middle East*, Praeger, 1967.

93

causes of their frustration [that is, not within themselves as individuals]. They prefer to put the blame on some scapegoat.'

If this is impossible and the frustration or shame cannot be rationalized then the Arab becomes neurotic, perhaps to the point of breakdown. Several Egyptians have told me seriously that President Nasser suffered so acutely from shame after the 1967 military defeat that it directly caused his death three years later.

In connection with the Israelis, stains on Arab honour and references to humiliation have become propaganda material. The Arab peoples are repeatedly told of the need to wash away such stains with enemy blood.

Two such examples suffice here:

'May 15, 1948, is a day that will never be forgotten in our history. It is the day of the outbreak of the Palestine war and the establishment of the State of Israel. This is the day of the greatest shame in the modern history of the Arabs.'*

'The armed forces are getting ready for the restoration of the rights of the Palestine People because the Palestine battle was a smear on the entire Arab Nation. No one can forget the shame brought by the battle of 1948.'†

It might be expected that in such a shame-oriented society suicide would be frequent. In fact, this is extremely rare, largely for reasons given by T. E. Lawrence, who found the desert Arabs a limited, narrow-minded people 'whose inert intellects lay fallow in incurious resignation. Their imaginations were vivid but not creative. . . . They could almost be said to have had no art . . . they had no organizations of mind or body. They invented no systems of philosophy. . . . They had accepted the gift of life unquestioningly, as axiomatic. To them it was a thing inevitable, entailed on man, beyond control. Suicide was a thing impossible. . . .'‡

* *Al-Ahram* editorial, May 15, 1964.
† Speech by President Nasser on August 11, 1963, reported in *Egyptian Gazette*, August 12, 1963.
‡ *The Seven Pillars of Wisdom*, Jonathan Cape, 1946, p. 36.

The disinclination to suicide even among urbanized Arabs is perhaps better understood if we compare them with, say, the Swedes or the Japanese, both races with a high suicide rate. In an over-simplified explanation, the Swede's and the Japanese's aggression is towards himself and when he cannot contain it he might commit suicide. The Arab's aggression is towards his neighbour, so introverted aggression is unlikely.

When a prominent Arab is said to have committed suicide it is almost certainly a case of political murder.

With his sensitivity to pride and shame it is not surprising that the Arab is easily offended. Western visitors would be astonished to know how frequently they unintentionally hurt Arabs with whom they have social or business connections. This can be seen when the Arab is trying to define a policy, political, ideological or economic. After an elaborate introduction he loses his main theme and becomes bogged down in detail. Rhetoric consumes him and his speech is full of similes and metaphors. His Western contact finds all this time-wasting and often embarrassing and he shows his reaction. The Arab is hurt by lack of appreciation of his eloquence and by what seem to him blunt replies.

Social situations can be fraught with difficulties. The Arab wants physical contact with the person with whom he is conversing, likes close face-to-face dialogue, and asks many personal questions. It is sometimes difficult for a Westerner to restrain his irritation with these intimacies. Again, in Arab society it is not rude to be late for an appointment. From Morocco to Iran I have waited hours to be collected 'precisely' at a certain time and I now realize that no offence has been intended. It is a simple matter of different values given to time.

All over the Arab world Western businessmen fume with impatience in hotel lobbies. The National Palace Hotel in Tripoli, Libya, is a good example. Each day men of a score of nationalities check in at the National Palace to begin negotiations to tap Libya's money-choked treasury. But what they expected to take a few days drags into weeks because of lost time. A car is to be sent at 8 a.m. and when it arrives at 11.30 a.m. the foreigner is exasperated enough to speak sharply to the Libyan official he has travelled thousands of miles to see. The man is instantly hurt and nothing constructive will be done that day.

Shame can result when an Arab is not treated as a 'special case'. Searching constantly for personal attention, he expects any rule to be bent to suit his convenience. And he expects to be the favourite. I have constantly had to assure Arab friends that each of them counts more with me than the others. On one occasion I interviewed two Arab terrorist leaders separately while the other waited in an outer office. Later the first interviewee, Hazim, said accusingly, 'You spoke to Nasir for five minutes longer than you spoke to me.' He was really hurt by this apparent slight and was mollified only when I explained that the extra time was necessary because of Nasir's inability to express himself as eloquently as Hazim.

It is so easy to give unintentional offence. By stretching the left hand towards a person's face, as one might do in casual gesticulation, would be tantamount to telling many an Arab that he has the evil eye and that your hand is used defensively against it.

If all this seems trivial I must say again that to apply Western culture-values to the Arab world is a mistake. To respect their pride and be aware of their shame works to the foreigner's advantage.

Arabs can be magnanimous and they appreciate generous people, but they expect generosity in return. A relationship is necessarily reciprocal and to accuse the Arab of being 'calculating' because he expects reciprocity in any arrangement is to judge him by alien standards. Even so, an Arab feels that a gift ought to be questioned on the assumption that an apparently selfless donor is not to be trusted. The Egyptians are especially suspicious. In a comparative study of students from ten countries, Gillespie and Allport* asked their subject to list

* James M. Gillespie and Gordon W. Allport, *Youth's Outlook on the Future* (Doubleday Papers in Psychology), Doubleday, New York, 1955.

three influential events in their lives. Egyptians mentioned more often than any others disagreeable experiences that engender distrust of people.

To the Westerner, the Arab is frustratingly inconstant. Sometimes he will interact intensely with others, and is volatile, emotional and perhaps fanatical; he responds to environmental stimuli. But he is equally capable of apathy and melancholia and will lapse into a sullen silence. At such times he is insensitive to his own or other people's sufferings. More often than not he will be undergoing an agony of shame in one form or another.

6 *As Arab Men See Women*

[handwritten margin note:] The men are made responsible for the women since God endowed them with certain qualities, and made them the bread earners. Righteous women will cheerfully accept this always and observe God's commandments, even when alone in their privacy. If you experience opposition from women. 1 you shall first Talk to them

[handwritten margin note:] 2 deserting them in bed 3 they you may do as a last alternative beat them (in self defence)

'Men have authority over women because Allah has made the one superior to the other, and because they spend their wealth to maintain them. Good women are obedient. They guard their unseen parts because Allah has guarded them. As for those from which you fear disobedience admonish them and send them to beds apart and beat them. Then, if they obey you, do nothing further against them.' Koran, sura iv: 'Women'.

'Woman became a machine for muscular exercise, while man's psychic side could be slaked only among his peers [in homosexuality].' T. E. Lawrence, *The Seven Pillars of Wisdom*.

The role of women in Arab society is responsible for some of the most chronic difficulties in the Arab mind. By denying equality of sex, Arab men have made love, companionship and friendliness impossible between men and women. For those Arabs who take the Koran seriously it is logically impossible to treat women more liberally; as the Koran has ordained, so must it be. Women are inferior. Of course, this is over-simplified. Changes *are* taking place in some parts of the Arab world, but they are so slow that generations must pass before sexual equality is recognized in the Western sense.

[handwritten margin note:] The Koran gives more right to women than US Constitution it said they are equal but different in their make up like USA

Because of the frustrations and repressions which follow from the rigidly held sexual mores and prohibitions of his own society, the Arab is dangerous to women of other nationalities. Many Western girls working for big companies with branches in Arab countries have been indecently assaulted or raped. It is impossible for a woman to walk down a public street at night without serious risk. It is difficult enough for her to drive a car

98

alone. Arab men in groups are constantly on patrol in their own cars, watching for such prey, in cities such as Beirut and Tripoli.

In the pre-Islamic society, the position of women was high and their influence great. They were free to choose their husbands, and, if ill-treated or displeased, they could return to their own people. In some cases they even offered themselves in marriage and had the right of divorce. They were regarded not as slaves and chattels, but as equals and companions. They inspired the poet to sing and the warrior to fight. Nicholson believes that the chivalry of the Middle Ages is, perhaps, traceable to heathen Arabia. Two other highly regarded orientalists, Lady Anne and Mr Wilfred Blunt, came to much the same conclusion. 'Knight-errantry, the riding forth on horseback in search of adventures, the rescue of captive maidens, the succour rendered everywhere to women in adversity—all these were essentially Arabian ideas, as was the very name of *chivalry*, the connection of honourable conduct with the horse-rider, the man of noble blood, the cavalier.'*

The nobility of the women is not only reflected in the heroism and devotion of the men; it is recorded in song, in legend, and in history.

It would be wrong to blame Mohammad and the Koran for the entire deterioration in the woman's position. The Koran might have ruled that woman was secondary to man but Mohammad is said to have behaved in an exemplary manner towards his wives. In Islam's first and second centuries Moslem women, in some areas, were treated with affection as trusted companions. Sheikh Hafiz Wahba, formerly Saudi Arabian ambassador in London, told me that 'unfortunately the moral and religious decay which has befallen Islam has also had its effects on women and on matrimonial relations'.

Sheikh Wahba said that on the whole the position of women in Nejd—that part of Saudi Arabia on the Persian Gulf—is better in the 1970s than in Kuwait and Bahrein, where so abject has their position become that when the word 'woman'

* *The Seven Golden Odes of Pagan Arabia*, London, 1903.

99

is mentioned in conversation the speaker usually feels he should excuse himself as if he had mentioned some inferior kind of animal. Some men go so far as to apologize after mentioning their mothers, but this custom is dying out and the younger generation of educated men seldom do it. Woman's position is such that, as has been previously discussed, when an Arabian family discovers a moral lapse on the part of one of its female members, their only remedy is the sword, often in circumstances of great cruelty, and the ruler makes no investigation, taking it for granted that the family was justified.

[margin note: Against God's law]

It is worth mentioning that in some towns in Oman women serve in the shops, and even welcome guests when their husbands are not at home. But the Oman people are much criticized for this in other parts of the Arab world, where, to the Arab man pregnancy and menstruation are defects in a woman and signs of inequality.

In public, a man often tries to show the opposite of love. He seeks to mislead the audience by pretending hatred, negative criticism and ridicule. If the woman is pleased with the advances that she reads in the teasing process, she must express a negative and disconcerted response. A proverb sums up this attitude whereby the Arab shows hatred in public towards the woman he loves—'If you hear him swear at her know that he loves her.'

Many scholars have drawn attention to the man versus woman nature of Arab society. A kind of war is in progress in which the men are the overt victors. But the women, as a downtrodden minority, have a cohesion that the men could never achieve—the cohesiveness of contempt, as expressed in the poem by Fadwa Touqan.

The whole complex situation is partly caused by the upbringing of the Arab boy. He is constantly told, and has the evidence of what he sees, that males are superior to females. But his father beats him frequently; at the age of forty many Arab men tremble in the presence of their elderly fathers. The boy can salve his own ego by beating with impunity his sisters and, in many Arab groups, his mother. Despite this, he dearly loves his

[margin note: how]

100

mother, who eases her hostility against her husband by pampering her sons. About the time when the boy's adoration for his mother is at its peak he is expected by tradition to enter the male world and exercise his male prerogative of superiority. He never really quite resolves all these cross-currents affecting his development.

His difficulties can be seen in the strict code which forbids discussion of sex between men and women, even between husbands and wives. It is a common topic, though, among men and among women when the other sex is not present. Many village families live in one or two rooms, so children inevitably see and hear much of sex, but they must restrain their inevitable curiosity and interest. Observers who have lived in villages report that children hear much sexual talk, from the women especially. Winifred Blackman,* who spent some time among the Upper Egyptians, says, 'Sexual matters form the chief topic of their conversation. . . .' Even in front of children adults 'discuss the most private matters without the slightest reserve', so that from their very early years children hear sexual matters 'spoken of and joked about'. But when they reach puberty boys and girls are placed under severe sexual restrictions.

Sexual relationships are dominated by male impulses. What Kazem Daghestani says of the Syrian husband may be extended to other Arabs as well. 'His jealousy derives from his pride and familial honour, rather than from love. His wife is his honour. It is his honour which would be injured if his wife misbehaved.' Precisely because the honour of husbands, fathers and brothers is tied up with a woman's sexual conduct, men are highly suspicious of women in this respect. They believe that women have strong sexual desires which they are too weak to control. Therefore, they must be carefully guarded for the combination of their impulses and weaknesses would soon disgrace their fathers and brothers and husbands. With this 'logic', women are justifiably secluded and confined to their own company. An effective way of preventing misconduct and of ensuring a

* *The Fellahin of Upper Egypt*, F. Cass, 1968.

marriage that would bring credit to the family has been child betrothal and marriage. A girl promised to a man early in life is under the surveillance of two families. By selecting her husband when she is young, the family reduces the likelihood that she will be able or even want to exercise her own judgment or preference.

Perhaps this is a rationalization for the subjection in which Arab men hold their women. It may also express their own sense of guilt since they are concerned mainly with their own gratification in sexual relations.

Arab men place great value upon their own sexual prowess. They boast of their virility, but they must be careful not to become victims, through their erring wives and unmarried daughters and sisters, of the virility of other men. The emphasis upon sexual 'ability' is in accord with early marriage, the practice of taking more than one wife, and easy divorce by the husband.

In recent years, in the cities and among the better-educated classes, marriage occurs later, polygamy is disappearing and divorce is subject to customary restrictions, all of which make women more nearly the equal of men and legitimately available to men under more restrictive conditions. But precisely because of such circumstances, the continued consecration of male sexual vigour has increased unsatisfied male desires to the point where sex is an obsession with many young men. Hamady has noticed that under the strict and restraining code, whenever an Arab man finds himself alone with a woman, he makes sexual approaches to her. A frequent topic among groups of Arab men is the 'total immorality' of Western women. When Arabs go abroad their projected sexual adventures loom more importantly than any work or study.

Sex is so important that the Bedouin, who are expert trackers, stress that they can not only distinguish between the trails of a man and a woman but can tell whether the woman is a virgin. A Bedouin has explained this to me but too crudely to be described here. Basically, a virgin walks differently.

No one can stay on good terms with an Arab if he wounds or slights his honour. The defloration of a virgin girl, the committing of adultery by a woman, or any association between a man and a woman, are sensitive subjects, since they cause long-standing enmities, wild anger, or, at worst, murder. In spite of their strong ideas of propriety and their sensitivity about their reputation, women make the *'ird* of other women the most delightful topic of gossip. They are expert in tearing apart each other's reputation and the resultant rumours spread like wildfire.

Arabs use much licentious, coarse and obscene language and indecorous gestures. A common form of abuse among women quarrelling over reputations is the *qahba, yâ bint 'l-harâm* (you slut, you daughter of sin).

They call the man *qawwâd*, a procurer who brings customers to prostitutes. This term is perhaps the lowest form of abuse of one man to another, and is bitterly resented.

Other resentments are less violently expressed. When I first travelled in Arab countries I sometimes took my wife with me to interviews so that she could take shorthand notes while I concentrated on the conversation. It was useful, too, to be able to compare impressions. We were soon to learn that this practice was a mistake. With my wife present the Arab, no matter how Westernized, was hesitant, evasive and even hostile. I was exposing him to shame should he be unable to answer a question. In any case a woman had no business taking part in a conversation between men. Even when my wife sat passive and silent throughout the interview the tension remained. When I later interviewed the same men alone the atmosphere was quite different.

The presence of so many Arabs living within Israel—the Israeli-Arabs as distinct from the Arabs of the West Bank—provides contrasts which are invaluable to the historian, sociologist and psychologist. For instance, a well-meaning group of Israelis in Jerusalem decided to arrange a party to be attended by an equal number of Israeli and Arab married couples, the object being to bring about some kind of social

103

communication and accord. On the night arranged the Israeli husbands and wives were disconcerted when all the Arab husbands arrived—without their wives. Quite without collusion, each Arab made some lame excuse; his wife was not well or her family had arrived unexpectedly or there was difficulty with the children. That was the first disaster. The second was the Arabs' idea of enjoying the party; they flirted with the Israeli wives. One of the organizers told me very sadly, 'I suppose we should have known better.'

The easy, comradely relationship between Israeli men and women causes other problems among the Israeli-Arabs. The sight of Israeli couples swimming together, walking arm in arm or embracing reminds them all too frustratingly of the prohibitions of their own society. More than this, the spectacle of Israeli girls in mini-skirts or bikinis is distracting to the point of not wholly concealed masturbation in public places. During the summer months many tens of thousands of Arabs cross into Israel from Jordan to see relations, and large numbers visit the beaches to enjoy the display of Israeli nubility. The only Arab women in sight are matrons clad from head to toe in their black gowns.

The changes in women's status are being forced by the women themselves, led by those who have been university trained, particularly if they have been abroad. This is the real revolution in the Arab world. More intelligent and more realistic than the men, these young women are prepared to forsake marriage for equality, if necessary. Their long-repressed personalities are finding an outlet in activities ranging from teaching to terrorism.

Men are subdued in their presence because they cannot run the risk of being bested in argument; such a blow to pride could never be lived down. The numbers of such women are small and nearly all live in Beirut and Tunis or in Israel; a few are struggling to establish themselves in Tripoli, Libya. It will be many years before they breach the male bastions of Damascus and Baghdad, where Koranic dictums about women are still observed to the letter. For instance, a man may not pray if he

104

has had 'intercourse with women while travelling' and cannot find water to wash his face and hands. He may, however, use clean sand and rub his face and hands with it. The meaning adduced by Koranic scholars is that women are certainly less than men if they must be 'washed off' before prayer, even if there is no injunction about washing the genitals. The same chapter, like many others, promises marriage with 'chaste virgins' in gardens watered by running streams to those men who have faith and 'do good works'. With such insistent Koranic emphasis on virginity it is no wonder that in the Arab world a married woman is inferior. I have asked many Arabs what happens to the virgins once they have lost their virginity in the gardens of paradise, which they must assuredly do very quickly. Are they then thrown out of paradise and fresh virgins brought in? Nobody has been able to give me an answer.

But it *is* known that political activities are a sex palliative and in some cases a form of sublimation. It is no coincidence that politics, from tribal to national level, are an indulgence and self-indulgence in Arab society. They are a way of taking the mind off the consuming pre-occupation with sex. In an extreme form the pre-occupation is expressed by going to near certain death in a coup against the establishment, in a factional fight, or an act of terrorism. Death in such an event would bring its own reward—the martyr would find himself among many beautiful, and more importantly, willing girls in paradise.

the Best is 33:35 for both men equality of Men and and women Women. according to Coran see 24:3 24:26 25:63 to 68

105

7 Violence—'The Most Positive Form of Prayer'

'For when we love our nation and our fellow-Arabs and wish them a prosperous future and a dignified life, we do not shrink from the use of force against all who attempt to hinder our progress and our evolution.' Michael 'Aflaq, co-founder of the Arab Socialist Resurrection Movement, *For the Sake of the Ba'th*, Beirut, 1959.

'The hatred which we indoctrinate into the minds of our children from their birth is sacred.' Syrian Minister of Education, Suleiman Al-Khash, in a letter to René Maheu, Director-General of UNESCO.*

'The attitude of perpetual revolt against every power which seeks to control his freedom is the key to the series of aimless crimes and treacheries which make up the greater part of Arab history. . . . This psychology must be borne in mind in the history of all dealings with Arabs.' De Lacy O'Leary, *Arabia And Mohammad*, London, 1922.

Perhaps the aspect of the Arab mind which is most difficult —and most important—for Western people to understand is the traditional and unceasing use of violence and cruelty whether it happens as the result of deliberation or spontaneous combustion. I am not speaking of the violence of Palestinian terrorists against Western airlines, offices, embassies, shops and individuals; information on this subject is available from many sources.† Nor do I propose to more than mention the terrorists' violence against other Arabs—a long catalogue of assassinations, factional murders, massacres and vicious assaults. The traditional nature of this kind of violence is indicated by the

* The letter was reproduced in *Al-Thaura*, the Ba'ath party newspaper, May 3, 1968.
† Including my book *Fedayeen: The Arab-Israeli Dilemma*, published in England by Cassell and in the United States by Free Press, 1973.

Arab writer Fawaz Turki: 'The Palestinian's consciousness is stuffed and devastated by images of violence—violence that a Palestinian grows up with like he grows up with his skin.'* I know personally of one Lebanese Arab who refused to allow terrorists to use his house; his widow told me how they cut his throat in front of his children. Again, such atrocities are commonplace and can be read in the Press.

The cruelty of Arab slavers is a matter of history. Arabs were the instigators of the African inter-tribal warfare in which black men were pitted against black men to obtain the captive slaves. Wherever the Arabs lived across the whole of Africa in lands bordering those of the black Africans they established a quasi-feudal hegemony. They were the overlords, the emirs, the white-robed horsemen, the dwellers in forts and palaces. And the slavers. As recently as 1956 I saw a slave market in Jiddah and slavery continued into the late 1960s, the slaves being bought by oil money from agents operating around Lake Chad.

Western soldiers who fought the Arabs were always trained to keep their last bullet for themselves—an insurance against the torture they inevitably faced. Men of the French Army caught by Arab foes in Morocco, Algeria, Tunisia or Syria were buried to their necks in sand to die in the blazing sun and were sometimes smeared with honey or jam to attract the ants. Bestial indignities were inflicted on captives before they were killed. When the Arabs captured a group of Frenchmen they would sometimes cut off their hands, shuffle them and leave them in odd pairs stuck in the sand in attitudes of prayer. To the disgust of the French, women were usually more barbarous than their men. We now know that the women were reacting against their own oppression by men of the tribe, a psychological distinction which would not have given the French soldier any consolation.

Again, this type of violence is historical. I am more concerned here with violence within Arab societies—violence as a

* 'To Be a Palestinian', an article in *Journal of Palestine Studies*, Vol. III, No. 3, 1974.

political solution, for instance—and since it would be repetitive to deal with all eighteen countries of the Arab League I shall deal mainly with the Iraqis, Syrians and Egyptians, omitting Algeria, where, during the war with France, 1954–62, many more Moslems were killed by other Moslems than by the French. But complex issues make the Algerian violence a special case.

Violence which forms a thread in the normal fabric of life is more revealing in an analysis of the Arab mind. Violence exists at every level of Arab life but those men in the West whose business it is to shape policies towards the Arab world need to see clearly two main features of Arab politics. They have been explicitly identified by Professor P. J. Vatikiosis.* One is the weakness, often absence, of political institutions as understood in the West. The second is the low-level or non-existence of political community. 'These phenomena together form a vicious circle and they make it difficult and often unprofitable to curb personal and parochial attitudes, desires and conflicts. The result at public level has been mutual distrust between state and citizens, rulers and subjects, ruler and ruled, subjects and subjects. Lack of trust undermines every public endeavour —social, economic, political, military.'

A concomitant of mistrust is rivalry—tribal feuds in the desert, family and village feuds in the settled areas, and inter-group hostility in the towns. Arab political writers constantly stress Arab contentiousness which they blame (with imperialism) for Arab failure to achieve total unity. Poverty and frustration —sexual, economic, political—are so pervasive that there is a great deal of what Morroe Berger calls 'free-floating hostility'.† He sees politeness as a means of maintaining enough distance to prevent aggressive tendencies from becoming actual. Hos-pitality and generosity ward off expected aggression.

Conflict is so frequently on the verge of breaking out that personal relations seem to be directed at avoiding or covering up the slightest tendency towards the expression of difference.

* *Conflict in the Middle East*, George Allen and Unwin, 1971.
† *The Arab World Today*, Doubleday, 1962.

Few informal opportunities exist for serious discussion o opposing beliefs without a display of intense animosity. Excep among a few highly educated members of an elite group, Arab do not discuss differences, or they do so with a bitterness that is constantly at or over the edge of violence.

There is nothing new about Arab violence. We have seen how the Islamic world was torn with strife and dissension. The great Khaldun noted that the 'Bedouin are a savage nation, fully accustomed to savagery and the things that cause it. Savagery has become their character and their nature. They enjoy it, because it means freedom from authority. . . . Furthermore the Bedouin are not concerned with laws, or with deterring people from misdeeds or protecting some people against others. They care only for the property they might take away from people through looting. . . . It is noteworthy how civilization always collapsed in places the Bedouin took over and conquered.'*

Had he lived in a latter era, Khaldun might well have observed that considering the exploitation by Turkish overlords during the Ottoman empire it was not surprising that the 'Moslem peasantry should have become cruel, treacherous and un-truthful'. It was left to the orientalist Doctor James Parkes to make the point.

In one sense, the Arab concept of cruelty is grotesquely simple: it is better to be unjust, the Arab thinks, than to have others cruel to him. It is a variation on the kill or be killed idea. All Arab poetry emphasizes this view of cruelty. At least one scholarly Israeli expert on the Arabs, Dr Joshua Porat, who is in no sense 'anti-Arab', believes that cruelty is a tradition brought about by poetry.

Since 1949 revolution and military take-over, nearly always with bloodshed and cruelty, have been the most prevalent mean of reaching power throughout the Arab world. Only one of the eighteen Arab states—Lebanon—can be considered a demo-cracy. Virtually all the others have one-party systems usually dominated by the army. Between 1948 and 1973 the Arab

* *The Muqaddimah*, op. cit.

world suffered thirty successful revolutions and at least fifty unsuccessful ones. The number of failures is more difficult to determine, since unsuccessful *coups d'état* often go unreported. With rare exceptions, revolutions have been carried out by army officers, and the turnover has been rapid. Other than President Nasser, no revolutionary leader remained in power longer than six years. One, Colonel Naef of Iraq, was in office only thirteen days.

Assassination is an accepted means of political expression. Between 1948 and 1973 twenty-two heads of state and prime ministers were murdered. Numerous unsuccessful attempts were made on the lives of other leaders. In all, more than seventy major political murders and numerous unsuccessful assassination attempts were recorded in those twenty-five years.

Another form of political violence is the breaking-off of diplomatic relations. On sixteen separate occasions between 1958 and 1973 Arab governments broke off relations with Arab sister states and in another five cases relations were suspended.

One of the products of Arab instability has been the incidence of large-scale arrests and occasional mass murder of civilians. These are some of the more bloody occasions:

March 1959: At least 2,426 Iraqis were killed in the wake of a military revolt. (My information from reporters of the Beirut newspaper *Al-Hayat*, who were present.)

February 1963: Revolution led to the murder of between 1,000 and 5,000 Iraqis. (My information from an official of the Iraqi Ministry of Information.)

January 1965: About 200 worshippers at the Great Mosque of Bani Omayya, Damascus, were machine-gunned by Syrian troops. The massacre was not disclosed until July 29, 1969, when *Al-Hayat* reported it.

March 1970: About 30,000 members of the El Ansar religious sect were killed on Aba Island in the Nile by Sudanese military forces. (Report by Amman Radio, January 12, 1971. Egyptian estimates put the figure at 'several thousand'.)

June 1973: Nazem Kazzar made an abortive coup in Iraq and 37 Iraqis were executed. (Iraqi press reports.)

Beyond all this, between 1948 and 1973, there were twelve inter-Arab wars and civil wars, the latter often involving external Arab states. Some had elements of racial strife, as in the case of Sudan. Others were based on religious differences, as in Lebanon. But most frequently the main reason was desire for power. Some of these wars were hideously brutal; in the Yemen civil war Egypt used poison gas against Yemeni tribesmen.

These are the bare facts. One needs to study the phenomenon of Arab violence through certain nations and case histories in an attempt to understand why such brutality and torture can exist.

SYRIA

We get a crystallized picture of the Syrians from T. E. Lawrence who thought that while they were admirers of the truth they did not seek it. Lawrence found the Syrians, like the Egyptians, helpless in dealing with abstract ideas and lazy-minded. Their ideal life was to achieve the ease in which to busy themselves with other people's affairs. 'From childhood they were lawless, obeying their fathers only from physical fear. . . .'

It is fear, though not always of the physical kind, which has dictated much Syrian violence. Plots, coups, counter-coups, assassinations and mass murders permeate modern Syrian history. The French had dominated the country for decades and when they relinquished control after World War II the Syrians were eager to seize the power they had for so long been denied. The first *coup d'état* was that of Colonel Za'im in 1949 and to underline his authority and to flush out any possible conspirators he used torture as a punishment for past transgressions, and as a warning against any future ones. Ironically, Za'im, having established a precedent for change of government by murder, was himself murdered. His coup was the first of three in 1949.

This was the time of the Ba'ath (Arab Social Renaissance)

111

Party, a radical group which used professional agitators to keep its activities prominent in the public mind. The Ba'ath, the Communist Party—Syria was the only Middle East country where the Communists operated legally—and several military factions were struggling for power. The Ba'ath and one of the anti-communist military groups resolved upon a merger of Syria with Egypt—the short-lived United Arab Republic. Disputes over this union caused one crisis after another and rival leaders succeeded one another first as rulers and then as prisoners.

Political prisoners were kept in Mezze gaol and subjected to barbaric tortures. The foolishness of inflicting torture on men who might the following week have the upper hand seemed not to occur to anybody. Alliances were unstable. For a while Ba'athists and Nasserites were partners but in 1963 they broke apart; both sides were plotting massacres but the Ba'athists struck first, killing hundreds of Nasserites in a series of well-organized surprise attacks. To give a semblance of legality to the anti-Nasserite hunts which followed, military courts were set up. Since no defence was permitted, the 'trial' was over in half an hour and victims were shot virtually on the spot.

The great Arab scholar, Aref el-Aref, drawing on a lifespan of eighty years when I interviewed him at his home in Ramallah in January 1972, told me that after the Iraqis the Syrians were the most 'introverted and xenophobic of Arabs'. But, as he saw it, their hatred and fear of foreigners extended to other Syrians outside their own social class, even those outside their immediate group. More important was their quick shift in allegiances which, for el-Aref, explained much Syrian violence. 'If today you turn against a man who was your friend yesterday you *must* act violently to rationalize your change. By being violent you are saying to yourself that this man did not deserve your friendship, that he has betrayed you and that he must be punished. He hates you so you must hate him. It is easy for many of us Arabs to make the decision to hate.'

Much evidence exists to show that Syrian cruelty is the product of hate. The best documented research concerns fifteen Israelis who at various times beginning with 1948 fell into Syrian hands. By 1963, when eight of them were returned to Israel, only one was in mental condition to give a coherent account of their sufferings and to restart a normal life. Another of the eight committed suicide in his parents' home in Tel Aviv a few months after his release. The remaining six are likely to spend their lives in mental institutions.

The Syrians refused to allow Red Cross representatives to visit the captives and United Nations officials were allowed to see them only when they were finally exchanged. Israel's repeated requests for information brought only Syrian denial of knowledge of their existence.

At Tadmor (Palmyra) three men were kept in a cell too low for them to stand upright, with no sanitary facilities and no ventilation apart from a small aperture at the bottom of the door, through which they took turns to breathe. They were not allowed to relieve themselves but were whipped on the soles of the feet—a practice known as *Falakot* to the Arabs—for defecating in the cell. After finishing their soup they used the empty tins as toilet bowls so as not to have to defecate on the floor, but next day the prison cook served the soup in the same contaminated mugs. 'There's no water for washing dishes in the desert,' they were told, 'so eat up what you released last night.'

Physical tortures included electric shock by wires clipped to tongue and penis; being tied naked in the sun and smeared with jam for the flies and wasps. In 1962 for the first time since 1956 the prisoners were allowed to wash their clothes. Mental agony was added by their being told that Israel persisted in refusing to have them back. One of the men, wounded when captured, was kept in solitary confinement for a year without treatment, until an Armenian became the prison doctor. Another, found by his goalers to have unusually acute hearing, had his head beaten against a wall until his ear-drums fractured.

A few of these Israelis had been kidnapped inside Israeli territory by Syrian Army raiders. One, of Syrian origin, had gone back to try to get his mother out. Another man was taken off a Finnish merchant vessel that put into a Syrian port. Only two of the men had been charged with breaking Syrian law. One served three months for illegally crossing the border, after which he was held permanently in a military prison. The other, a Yemeni caught in 1947 trying to help Syrian Jews flee to Palestine, was sentenced to ten years' imprisonment; in 1957, instead of being released, he was sent to Tadmor, where in 1961 he died of his tortures.

From time to time the Israelis had the company of Syrians in misfortune. These were mainly of the Druze minority, generally suspected of being anti-Ba'athist. If anything they were treated even more cruelly than the Israelis. One, allegedly for spying, had all his fingernails and toenails torn out. Many of the men committed suicide in prison.*

Three Israeli airmen released by the Syrians in June 1973 in exchange for five senior Syrian officers and forty-one soldiers were tortured with beatings and electric shocks throughout their three years' captivity. An Air Force captain who broke a leg while landing by parachute was beaten on this leg, as subsequent medical examination showed. During the fourth Arab–Israeli War, in October 1973, the Syrians stabbed and mutilated about fifty Israeli soldiers before shooting them; when found by United Nations officers their hands had been bound with wire.

The plight of the 3,500 Jews of Damascus, Aleppo and Qamishli, the remnant of a once thriving community in Syria, is more serious than that of any other Jewish population in the world. In Damascus I have seen their ghettos, with doors opening into large interior courtyards where police and terrorists keep them under a 24-hour watch. Under oppressive restrictions, they would starve but for private American charity. The Syrians keep them as possible scapegoats or as a ransom should Israel capture high-value Syrians. Rape of Jewish girls

* Much of this information comes at first hand from Syrians who were in prison at the same time; it is corroborated by Egyptian officers held briefly after Syria broke away from her short-lived union with Egypt as the United Arab Republic.

by Syrian soldiers is common and torture is not rare. The London *Observer* reported in May 1974 that Syrian security officers had arrested eleven Syrian Jewish women in Aleppo and tortured them until they revealed the names of people helping to smuggle Jewish children out of Syria.

A basic psychological reason for Syrian violence and hostility is that the Syrian holds fiercely to his opinion and would like to impose it on everyone. If people disagree with him he will consider them inimical and intrigue against them. Again, the Syrian (and the Lebanese) likes to know the private lives of others and will try to correct their 'errors'. Jamil Saliba, a Syrian scholar living in Egypt, says that this interference 'which ostensibly aims at correcting evil, is in many people the result of jealousy and hatred. The Syrian would like to see his neighbour happy but not successful. . . . He will try to cause the downfall of a successful neighbour in order to step into his place.'* Further, in Syrian society a successful man will rarely encourage a beginner and a beginner will rarely exalt the successful man.

Brutality is often a public spectacle. The most bizarre instance in decades was the execution of the Israeli spy, Elie Cohen, who became a close friend of the Syrian president, General al-Hafez, in the early 1960s. Caught in the middle of a broadcast to Tel Aviv, Cohen was hanged in public, on 'live' television, on March 5, 1965. The manner of Cohen's death, a Syrian journalist explained to me, was commensurate with the degree of shame he had brought to the Syrian hierarchy. Al-Hafez was one of six Syrian heads of state overthrown between 1949 and 1973; three of them were murdered.

IRAQ

Of all Arab countries Iraq has been most subject to violence in modern times with fifteen known coups or abortive coups and assassinations between 1950 and 1973, and exhibitions of

* *Trends of Thought in Syria and Lebanon*, Institute of Higher Arabic Studies, Arab League, Cairo, 1958.

medieval barbarity equalled only in Uganda and Haiti. Assassination and terror are seen as legitimate political methods; elimination of possible rivals is accepted practice. Whichever party rules it has a list of victims—an administrative list—for murder is systematized. No man can stay on top without murder.

A basic problem is that Iraqis are not homogeneous. The indigenous Iraqis learnt to be cruel from the invading Mongols. 'Wounded in their pride, the Arabs of Iraq evinced from the first a turbulent, seditious, anarchical and in a word, a very Arab spirit. The province soon became a focus for political firebrands—the haunt of brigands and assassins.'*

For centuries these Iraqis persecuted the Arabs of the southern regions, thus making these people suspicious and hostile. In recent years Iraqi cruelty has been directed against the Kurds of the north and against the Iranians in the border lands. But violence is commonplace among Iraqi peasants; they are desperately poor and living in such conditions of oppression and frustration that murder is a form of relief.

This has long been the case, right from the days when the sheikhs were all-powerful. Every sheikh surrounded himself with a body of armed ruffians from his own tribe to act as his bodyguard and keep the peasants in subjection. Supported by these armed forces, the official police force, and the government machinery, the sheikhs were able to control the peasants. No one dared to complain or tried to prevent the sheikh from stealing his produce or refused to work on his land. The punishment would have been prison, torture or exile. Some sheikhs in the south had insect-infected prisons, into which their victims would be thrown to be flogged, and tortured by the sheikh's ruffians until they promised again to obey the master. A sheikh once visited his estate and stayed at the house of one of his peasants. The two quarrelled over some question of land rights and the peasant dared to raise his voice. The sheikh departed in a rage and the peasant sought refuge with a

* R. Dozy, *Essai sur l'histoire de l'Islamisme*, 1879.

friend whom he asked to mediate. After much bargaining, the sheikh agreed to pardon his peasant if he would pay him a sum that amounted to double the peasant's yearly income.*

With such a history of violence the murders in July 1958 of King Faisal II, Prince Abd al-Ilah, who was the Crown Prince, other members of the Royal Family, and Prime Minister Nuri Said, were hardly surprising, Many lesser people died in this uprising led by Brigadier Qassem and the blood-lust and blood-bath which followed were no more remarkable than other massacres in Iraq's history. The mutilation and defilement of Prince Abd al-Ilah's body are matters of historic record. As so often happens in Arab countries, the director of the coup and the new dictator, Qassem, met the fate of his principal victim. He had made himself a general and he was surrounded by guards but the year after his coup he was badly wounded in an assassination attempt. As usual, fierce and indiscriminate reprisals followed, yet less than five years after taking power Qassem lost it. The most suitable day for a military coup in an Arab country is Friday, the Moslem sabbath, especially during the holy month of Ramadan when most people are off their guard. Qassem's regime was overthrown on Friday, February 8, 1963, and it coincided with the 14th of Ramadan. The plotters, led by former close friends, had him executed at once, and his crushed body was shown on television. This display was calculated to inflame feelings against those people alleged to be pro-Qassem and massacres took place all over Iraq. The National Guard, a Ba'ath organization, provided the murder squads but when they met strong opposition they called in the army. The purge was worse than anything Iraq had yet endured.

Racial and religious rivalries, deep political enmities and personal antagonisms account for much of Iraq's violence. A heterogeneous country, its population is slightly over one-half Shii Arab, about 30 per cent Sunni Arab and about 20 per cent Sunni Kurdish. This mixture is overlaid with Pan-Arab, Iraqi-

* From Mohammed Tawfig Husayn, an Iraqi teacher of history at the American University of Beirut.

Nationalist, anti-American and even pro-Western groups; in addition, there are several rival factions of the Ba'ath Party (which had spread from Syria), the Communists and various military cliques. The innumerable permutations of alliances made possible by all these groups accounts to some extent for the violence which is woven into Iraqi life.

A psychological reason has been perceived by many foreign observers who have lived in Iraq. They say that in this patriarchal society, where junior members of the family are not allowed to make decisions and where junior army officers are made sharply aware that their opinion has absolutely no weight, grievances build up to the explosion point. Younger men, long denied their say, violently insist on it. The result is revolution and murder. Other observers say that Iraq's two languages—one idiomatic, the other literary—create a more dangerous mental ambivalence than in other Arab countries. The mind cannot come to terms with the two voices it is hearing.

A sudden introduction to the twentieth century is another deep-rooted cause of violence. Despite its memories of high civilization in the days of Sumer, Babylon, Assur and down to the Baghdad caliphate of the great monarch Haroun al-Rashid, 786–809, Iraq became one of the most stagnant areas of the Ottoman Empire. Not until late in the 1950s were the first efforts made to establish a modern university in Baghdad—suddenly Iraq had a student population which has not yet found its feet. Without a tradition of scholarship, these students are inevitably unstable and easily led.

The rapidity with which a violent situation develops has startled many travellers in Iraq, and all the more when the violence is dedicated to Allah. The mobs which periodically run riot in Baghdad, Basra and Mosul continually shout 'Allah is great!' This chanting is what so many foreigners most vividly recall about Baghdad's 'night of long knives' in June 1941. Encouraged by pro-Nazi agitators to revolt against the British, the citizens of Baghdad saw that to attack the British directly was suicidal so they savaged the Jewish community, all of whom were as much Iraqi as Jewish. Without interference from the Iraqi police or army, the rioters killed 179 Jews and wounded 2,118 more. They stripped 2,371 Jewish shopkeepers of their stock and 48,584 Jews lost all their possessions. Only the intervention of Kurdish units which came into the city saved the Jews from even greater losses. Of the 250,000 Jews in Iraq in 1941 fewer than 3,000 remain—and they are kept as a form of insurance. They can be used as levers against Israel and periodically some are rounded up and executed as spies. One of the most recent incidents of this kind occurred on January 27, 1969, when nine Jews and five other people were hanged in Baghdad and Basra. Hundreds of thousands of Iraqis converged on Baghdad's Liberation Square to view the bodies dangling on the gallows; large parties of school children were taken to view the scene.

Cruelty to the Kurds is not so well-publicized, perhaps because evidence is hard to get. But at least one case, that of Majid Hamid, of Darband, is thoroughly attested. In March 1970 the Iraqi Government signed an agreement with the Kurds with the declared object of bringing to an end the long war between them. But the Ba'athist regime implemented few of the agreement's clauses and did its best to split the Kurds and destroy their unity. The Kurds for some time honoured the agreement and even instructed their men to return to the service of the Iraqi Government and Army. One of them was Majid Hamid, a sergeant in the Iraqi Army. On May 5, 1972, Ahmed Hamid, the 75-year-old father of Majid, received a telegram informing him that his son was sick in hospital in Kut, and that he should visit him at once. Immediately Ahmed left for Kut where he arrived the following day. At a police checkpoint a security policeman was waiting for him and accompanied him on the pretext that he had been sent by Majid. The policeman took Ahmed to the Military Intelligence headquarters where he was arrested. There he learned that his son, too, had been arrested for an undisclosed reason. Blindfolded, the two were transferred separately to the Intelligence Directorate in Baghdad and from there to Al-Nahaya Palace.* Ahmed was kept there for three months and was not allowed to see his son. The two were then transferred to the central prison at Abu Gharib, where Ahmed was tried by a 'revolutionary court' which ordered his release on the grounds of insufficient evidence and his age.

Ahmed returned to his village worried over the fate of his son. Two weeks later he received a letter from his son saying that on September 1, 1972, prisoners were allowed to see visitors. Majid asked his father to bring him a Koran, a prayer rug and bedding. Ahmed, accompanied by his wife and Majid's wife, who had been married to him for only ten months, went to the prison and stood among the large crowd of prisoners' relatives waiting at the entrance to the prison. There they were recognized by someone who informed them that Majid had died as a result of torture three days before and that his body was in the hospital. He told them to claim the body before it was buried by the municipality, as is usual with the poor.

The family hurried to the hospital where they found Majid's body with his limbs slashed, his fingernails torn off, his eyes gouged out, his body full of stab wounds and burns made by an electrical instrument. Ahmed returned with his grieving family to their village, taking with him the body of his son which was examined by a foreign doctor and photographed before burial. This was the result of foresight by a Kurdish teacher and a friend of the murdered man. It is not the only incident of its kind but it is one of the few which a Western writer could advance with the confidence that the details are true. It must be admitted that the Kurds would deal no more gently with Iraqis in certain circumstances. For instance, in April 1974 the Kurds shot dead nineteen captive Iraqi officers as a reprisal after the Baghdad regime had executed eleven prominent Kurds the previous week.

Enmities in this part of the Arab world seem to be deeper than, say, in Tunisia or Libya. This deep-seated hostility was

* *Al-nahaya* means 'terminus'—the end.

shown at the end of October 1973. Iraq had sent military forces to aid Syria in her campaign against Israel but when Syria accepted a ceasefire Iraq withdrew these forces in protest. The Syrians were glad to see them go for large numbers of Syrian troops had been occupied in watching the Iraqis for signs of 'treachery'. Intense hatred exists between the rival left-wing regimes of the two countries, and the Syrian leaders suspected an Iraqi plot against them. The Iraqi anti-Israel contingent was heavily escorted until it had crossed the border on the way back to Baghdad.

While it is impossible to feel any tolerance for a regime which rules by terror we must have some sympathy for a people whose whole tradition is one of violence. They know no better. Their skin of culture and self-restraint is thin and is readily pricked by rabble-rousers. The Iraqi Arab, like most other Arabs, is easily goaded into wild passions.

EGYPT

An Egyptian social scientist has said that Arab society as a whole has 'an excess in personal feelings' which makes the individual consider a difference in opinion a personal insult.*
This is obvious in Egypt where these insults affect large groups, not only individuals. During the 1882 Urabi rebellion a Western observer wrote, 'In a Mohammadan country threatened by a Christian power any patriotic sentiment which may exist in the people has always a tendency to transform itself into religious fanaticism and in Egypt the transformation was systematically encouraged by the nationalist leaders.'†

The nationalist leaders always presented any foreign intervention as an insult to Mohammad and to Allah, a tactic which roused passions even in docile Egyptians.

In Egypt tensions are almost palpable, even in family groups, and quickly rise to explosion point. But the violence of the

* Hanna Rizk, 'The Individual and Society' in *Arab Society*, Institute of Arab Studies, American University of Beirut, 1953.
† D. Mackenzie Wallace, *Egypt and the Egyptian Question*, London, 1883.

Egyptian is different from that of the Syrian or Iraqi; it is directed inwards more than towards others.

An Egyptian journalist, Ahmad Lutfi al-Sayyid (1872–1963), was apparently aware of this inner conflict when he wrote that the most important fact about Egyptian history and that which explained the moral condition of her people was that she had always been ruled by force. Egyptians had to pretend to a loyalty they did not possess and lost their inner freedom, their courage, their moral link with the government. Violence was part of life.

The Ottoman Turks are largely responsible for the perpetuation of violence and the continuing acceptance of it by the Egyptians. Under the Turks, the Arabs viewed authority as a power traditionally accompanied by harshness and violence; the major role of the government was to exact taxes from them. The great mass of the people despised the compassionate ruler and delayed paying their taxes until they were beaten. Any man who paid up without being thrashed or tortured was treated with contempt by his neighbours. In time, the Arabs, and particularly the Egyptians, came to associate violence with authority. They still do.

Significantly, Colonels Naguib, 1952, and Nasser, 1954, were the first Egyptians in nearly 2,500 years to rule the land of the Nile. From the times of Cambyses and Alexander the Great, throughout the reigns of ancient Persia, Greece, Rome, the Byzantine Empire, the Arabs, Mamelukes, Turks, French and the British until the middle of the twentieth century—the rulers of Egypt were always foreigners. The Turks had made the Egyptians servile but the occupation of Egypt in 1798 by Napoleon Bonaparte brought the greatest changes. French rule was brief but profoundly significant; it began the period of direct Western intervention in the Arab world, with great economic and social consequences. With their easy victory the French broke the deep-seated illusion that the Islamic world could not be challenged by the infidel, inferior West. This created an enormous problem of readjustment and engendered psychological disorders which have not yet been resolved.

After so much foreign domination it was not surprising that the Egyptians gave Nasser the adoration due to a saviour. For his part, Nasser had been deeply influenced by two other saviours—Hitler and Mussolini; Nazi and Fascist ideology was ready-made for Egypt. It reassured the wealthy pashas who were making fortunes out of World War II; but it also provided a form of superficial socialism which hypnotized the masses of the poor, the ignorant and those easily taken in by slogans. The totalitarian doctrine had something for every Egyptian For young Lieutenant Nasser there were heady ideas of military victories as demonstrated by the Wehrmacht and Luftwaffe. He hoped for a geographical and political arena in which Egypt might become a new and proud power.

'When I went with the Egyptian delegation to the Kingdom of Saudi Arabia to offer condolences on the death of its great sovereign (Faisal) my belief in the possibility of extending the effectiveness of the Pilgrimage, building upon the strength of the Islamic tie that binds all Moslems, grew very strong. . . . In my mind's eye I saw all the regions of the world which Islam has reached. Then I found myself saying that our view of the Pilgrimage must change. . . . It should become an institution of great political power and significance. . . . When I consider the 80 million Moslems in Indonesia, and the 50 million in China, and the millions in Malaya, Siam and Burma, and the nearly 100 million in the Middle East, and the 40 million in the Soviet Union—together with other millions in far-flung parts of the world—when I consider these hundreds of millions united by a single creed, I emerge with a sense of the tremendous possibilities which we might realize . . . enabling them and their brothers in faith *to wield power precisely and without limit.'**

* *Egypt's Liberation: The Philosophy of the Revolution,* Public Affairs Press, Washington, 1952. My italics.

Nasser regarded the regime he ruled as revolutionary. July 23, 1952, was the beginning of a new historical era no less than July 14, 1789 (beginning of French Revolution), and November 7, 1917 (Russian Revolution). But there is a basic difference between the French and Russian Revolutions, when the masses rose up, and the Egyptian revolution, where the masses were passive. Lenin was the leader of an experienced, dynamic party. But Nasser and Naguib found themselves a vanguard without an army. Nasser wrote,

'Then suddenly came reality after July 23rd. The vanguard performed its task and charged the battlements of tyranny . . . Then it paused, waiting for the serried ranks to come up in their sacred advance towards the great objective. For a long time it waited. Crowds did eventually come, and they came in endless droves—but how different is the reality from the dream! The masses that came were disunited, divided groups of stragglers. The sacred advance was stalled. . . . We set about seeking the views of leaders of opinion and the experience of those that were experienced. Unfortunately, we were not able to obtain very much. *Every man we questioned had nothing to recommend except to kill someone else* [my italics]. If anyone had asked me in those days what I wanted most, I would have answered promptly: to hear an Egyptian speaking fairly about another Egyptian; to sense that an Egyptian has opened his heart to pardon, forgiveness and love for his Egyptian brethren.'

Nasser's tone seems to imply surprise that Egyptian individuals wanted to kill other Egyptian individuals and that unity was lacking. Yet this has been the pattern of Egyptian society for generations. Nasser had a vision or theocratic dream of an Arab future based on the status of Islam as a state religion. The Egyptians around him could see only as far as their own enmities, to be resolved in violence. And Nasser himself was soon using violence to further his dream, sending persuaders or assassins to deal with those who challenged Egypt's right to might. One of his victims was the Lebanese publisher Kamal Muruwa who had been rash enough to write, 'Each time a coup d'état occurs in an Arab country one is sure of finding the hand of Egypt there, either stirring it up, sustaining it or lending it support. But as soon as she succeeds she comes out against it and is bent on demolishing it, inciting another rebellion to balance it.' Muruwa ran his article, 'O Arabs of Sound Minds, Unite!' in his own paper, *Al-Hayat*, on September 22, 1963. Nasser warned him that he was 'dangerously right of centre', but Muruwa persisted in his efforts to check what he considered as destructive Egyptian intrigue. He was murdered in his office in 1965.

The earlier writings of Salama Musa and Taha Husayn were no more popular with Nasser. Musa had advised Egyptians to 'turn their faces towards Europe', a suggestion that brought bitter attacks. He was accused of retarding the progress of Arab consciousness and of turning Arab youth against their own society. Husayn urged his countrymen to believe that there was no difference between Egyptians and Europeans. 'Our real national duty, once we have obtained our independence and established democracy in Egypt, is to spend all we have and more, in the way of strength and effort, of time and money, to make Egyptians feel, individually and collectively, that God has created them for glory not ignominy, strength not weakness, sovereignty and not submission, renown and not obscurity, and to remove from their hearts the hideous and criminal illusion that they are created from some other clay than Europeans, formed in some other way, and endowed with an intelligence other than theirs.'*

Husayn's writings were branded as 'traitorous and anti-Islam', the second epithet being calculated to disgrace him utterly.

Violence in Egypt is sporadic rather than endemic as in Iraq but at higher levels nine major coups, abortive coups and

* From an essay in Arabic, Cairo, 1938.

assassination attempts are known; two attempts were made on Nasser's life. The largest abortive plot—by the Moslem Brotherhood in August 1965—led to the arrest of 8,000 people and numerous executions.

The Egyptians treated their Israeli prisoners, from the October 1973 war, with studied brutality. Some were left without food and water until they begged for it—in some cases as long as 48 hours. One 19-year-old soldier was kept alone in a small cell and beaten incessantly. Lieutenant Colonel Assaf Yaguri, the most senior Israeli officer held, was beaten several times on his way to a prison, where Lysol was poured into his open wounds and those of others. A 19-year-old private had one of his eyes smashed out with a rifle butt. The Egyptians laughed and said, 'Now you will look like General Dayan.'

A second Israeli was whipped by Egyptian interrogators. The doctor who treated him found fifteen linear scars on his back and deep ulcers on his wrists—caused by phone wires which bound him for fifteen days. Another young soldier, forced to sit on hot concrete, was later treated for third-degree burns. Yet another was beaten on the top of the feet with a rifle butt, causing great pain and later ulcers. A fourth soldier, on release, was treated for a broken pelvis, the result of a beating with a wooden club.*

Much violence is directed against Egyptian Christians—the Copts. Though a loyal people, they are an oppressed minority and collectively they have lost much of their property. Christians are often beaten up for no other reason than that they *are* Christian and the police rarely take action against the thugs.

In Egypt violence is handed on from father to eldest son to youngest son to the family donkey or dogs. Egyptian children can be unbelievably cruel to animals, but they are not conscious of cruelty. Such a concept is alien to them. They are simply doing what traditionally they have a right to do. As an Egyptian teacher, partly trained in the United States, told me, 'Every

* Most of this information from Dr Benjamin Fisher, a Canadian skin specialist working in a Tel Aviv hospital.

person needs to be master of somebody or some thing. Without this how could he ever feel any confidence?'

I have observed the Egyptian passing-on of violence many times. On one occasion I was a guest in a house where the youngest son, aged five, was slapped by his father, though not harshly, for consistently interrupting the adults while they were speaking. The little boy wandered around the house sullenly until he found a servant at the top of the stairs—so he pushed him down the stairs. The family was vastly amused; the father called the boy and ruffled his hair affectionately. The servant, though he had a rough, bruising fall, showed no sign of resentment and I doubt if he felt any.

In rural Egypt no person of any standing or wealth would walk far from his home without an armed guard in front and another behind, both men with hands constantly on the triggers of their weapons. At the homes, surrounded by a tall wall, a guard is constantly on duty and at night savage dogs are released to patrol the grounds until daybreak. Violence, in short, is only averted by the unceasing threat of counter-violence, a philosophy and practice that reaches from President to fellah.

JORDAN

It would be a mistake to omit Jordan from an examination of Arab violence for this country has been the root of so much turmoil since 1948. Almost the cradle of violence in the modern Middle East, Jordan became a nursery for Palestinian terrorists and for *agents provocateurs* from other Arab countries. For instance, Egypt and Syria backed an abortive military plot in February 1958; in July 1960 the Syrian Deuxième Bureau (Intelligence Department) sponsored another plot to overthrow the regime; the Ba'ath Party sent agents from Syria and Iraq to make yet another attempt, also abortive. Apart from these external attempted coups others have been organized or part-organized from inside Jordan. After the Palestine War of 1948,

King Abdullah's army, spearheaded by the Arab Legion, held most of the Arab-populated parts of Palestine, including Old Jerusalem and the so-called West Bank. Abdullah then annexed eastern parts of Palestine—those on the opposite side of the Jordan. This action, considered high-handed by other Arab countries, led to his assassination by followers of the Mufti of Jerusalem, Haj Amin al-Husseini.

The new territories gave Jordan a population equally divided among resident Palestinians, Bedouins, and refugees from parts of Palestine included in the state of Israel. The mixture was volatile and since most groups felt they had a grievance against King Hussein, who had succeeded to the throne in 1952, he was a frequent target for assassination; between 1951 and 1975 at least twelve attempts were made on his life. Some of his ministers were murdered, chiefly Prime Minister al-Majali and ten of his entourage in August 1960.

It should be remembered that despite Jordanian government propaganda which purports to trace the country's history back to somewhere near the beginning of the Christian era, Jordan (originally Transjordan) was created as a British mandate after World War I. As Transjordan, it did not lose its mandate status until after World War II.

The Middle East scholar Dankwart A. Rustow of the City University of New York has said* that Jordan has the most artificial boundaries, the poorest endowment in natural resources and the least-developed feeling of civic loyalty of any country in the Middle East.

A state formed by drawing lines on a map, Jordan was bound to develop tensions and violence, since its subjects were of Syrian, Saudi Arabian, Iraqi, Lebanese, Palestinian and Bedouin origin and its central position made the country a nest of intrigue.

From the beginning of Mandate days provocateurs were bent on creating trouble. The original focus was against Britain but in a country with Jordan's economic, social and educational

* *Hussein: A Biography*, Barrie and Jenkins, London, 1972.

frustrations any excuse for violence was welcomed. This was especially so among the Palestinians, for they were better educated than other Jordanians, whom they regarded as ultra-conservative and reactionary.

Aref el-Aref, who spent much of his long life in Jordan, considered that 'violence is bred into the Jordanian by his mother and nurtured by every adult he encounters.' He believed that the rapid growth of Amman—from a desert outpost to a metropolis of 300,000 people in a generation—was responsible for much of Jordan's violence. 'The Arab,' he said, 'is acutely responsive to the pressures around him, and in Amman those pressures are new and raw.'

Jordanian violence itself is raw and as the so-called Civil War of 1970 showed it could reach massive proportions. In this war, with the Jordanian Army on one side and Palestinian terrorists on the other, possibly 10,000 Arabs died; some estimates say 20,000. Many more died during the next twelve months as King Hussein's forces drove remnants of the terrorist forces out of the country. The bitter feelings engendered by this conflict led to the assassination in Cairo, in November 1971, of Jordan's Prime Minister, Wasfi el-Tel. One of his killers licked up his blood.

King Hussein's biographer, Peter Snow, sees little hope of peace in Jordan: '. . . Reason comes hard to the Arabs, who blame Hussein as much as Israel for their present helplessness in defeat, and if Hussein has a vision of a land that will one day be reunited, peaceful and free of political turmoil it is a dream that will probably not be fulfilled in his lifetime'.*

Violence has become a commodity. It was always exportable within the Arab world but in modern times it reaches further afield and has the more open sanction of governments and political leaders.

In May–June 1974, when the American Secretary of State, Henry Kissinger, visited Damascus on one of his many attempts

* In *Middle Eastern Political Systems*, Prentice-Hall, 1971.

to secure a separation of Syrian and Israeli forces on the Golan Heights, no fewer than five assassination squads were known to be out to kill him. Three had been sent by terrorist organizations, one was controlled by a Moslem religious group and another was under Libyan orders. Libya has made no secret of its violent means to violent ends. Colonel Qaddhafi's commitment to Islamic revival is linked in his mind with the need for a 'third theory'—subversion for its own sake—to combat Communism and imperialism; the nation's vast oil revenues finance crusades of violence. The target areas are the Maghrib (Arab west) and Mashriq (Arab east) and Middle East. In the Maghrib, Morocco, with its U.S. links, is a natural target; Libya trains large bands of men for incursions into Morocco and has financed assassination attempts. In the Mashriq, Libya has given sanctuary and much money to terrorists. Libyans have plotted to kill King Hussein and have financed riots in several Syrian towns to overthrow the Ba'athist regime. Lebanon has frequently protested that Libya is running in arms for use in coups. Indeed, few countries in the Middle East and Africa have escaped the Libyan doctrine of violence.

Even in Egypt, Qaddhafi ordered and paid for what he hoped would be a major coup. He engaged Dr Ibrahim Abdullah Sariyah, a 38-year-old Palestinian, to arrange an attack on the army engineering school in Cairo. Sariyah had already led the terrorist party which massacred thirty people of mixed nationality at Rome airport in December 1973. Qaddhafi was interested in the Egyptian exploit as an experiment in establishing terror groups within all Arab states so that he could give teeth to any threat he made against his Arab neighbours. The purpose of the raid on the engineering school was to steal arms and then arrest President Sadat. The raid was abortive but eleven people, mostly civilians, were killed—by knives, Assassin-style. Ironically, only months before the attack, Qaddhafi was trying to woo Sadat into a union of Libya and Egypt. Political friendships are tenuous in the Arab world.

By Arab tradition, violence in act, attitude and language

produces the quickest results. 'Violence,' a Libyan cabinet minister told me, 'is the Moslem's most positive form of prayer.'

In some countries violence is positively *part* of prayer. In Saudi Arabia the powerful religious police—the *matowa*—enforce the closure of all businesses during prayer time and coerce people into the mosques. People late for a prayer session are beaten with sticks. The Saudis also deal roughly, and no doubt effectively, with criminals. After the third offence for theft the right hand is lopped. This is even more cruel than it seems; Saudis eat only with the right hand as the left hand is considered 'unclean', so for the rest of his life the amputee will have to eat alone.

Violence has never been far from a ruler in Saudi Arabia and in March 1975 King Faisal was shot dead by an assassin, one of Saudi Arabia's 3,000 princes and said to be deranged. Only a few months before, King Faisal had been nominated by *Time* Magazine as its "Man of the Year" but neither domestic nor foreign reputation protects the Arab ruler indefinitely. Despite his oil wars, Faisal appeared to many a pillar of pro-Western views and a focus of Arab moderation, at least in regard to the West. On his succession, King Khaled doubled the strength of the royal bodyguard, while experienced observers of the Saudi Arabian scene predicted that the nation could be heading towards the beginning of the end of the 70-year-old monarchy and yet another nucleus of instability in the Middle East.

The Westerner is stupefied by Arab violence. After a Palestinian terrorist attack he will say, 'But it's all so senseless!' This is to expect something logical from the fundamentally irrational. When projected outwards Arab violence is non-selective; the identity of the victims is immaterial. For the Arab, violence in itself is consolatory.

8 *Arabs Speaking of Arabs*

'The obstacles in the way of Arab nationalism are poverty, disease, ignorance, dependence on others, the absence of a sense of responsibility, the adoption of corrupt and corrupting political and economic governmental systems, acquiescence to tyranny, the all-too-easy idolatry practised towards rulers, kings and so-called leaders, strongmen and prominent personalities before one has had time to test them.' George Hanna, A Christian-born Arab, *The Meaning of Arab Nationalism*, Beirut, 1959.

'Arab nationalism was embodied in [the Arab's] gentleness, love of peace and hatred of violence, coupled with a proper self-respect, aversion to injustice, and refusal to tolerate any insult or injury to Arab dignity.' Dr Ibrahim Juma'a, *Ideology of Arab Nationalism in Emergence from the Consciousness of the Arabs*, Cairo, 1960.

As a preface to this chapter it is helpful to take notice of the existence of the large number of Arabophiles in the Western world and examine their feelings. Some diplomats who have served in Arab countries, oil men, engineers and teachers, return to their countries with affection for the Arabs. Several have told me that they are 'violently pro-Arab', a phrase which I suspect in many cases to mean nothing more than that they are anti-Israel. The question, 'What do you particularly admire in the Arab character?' produces evasive, ambivalent or ambiguous answers. 'The Arab is good company, if you know how to treat him'; or 'I envy the desert Arab his total freedom'; or 'The Arab has a dignity we have lost, though he's tiresome when he loses it.'

On examination, the basis of the Westerner's respect for the

Arab seems to be pity for his plight. This especially is so in the case of the Englishman, who has always been generous to the lame; one always feels satisfaction in helping people unable to help themselves.

The word 'sympathy' in its various connotations, but usually in the same patronizing tone, recurs in what Arabophiles write and say. 'Thousands of British people were bound by personal links of love and sympathy with individual Arabs,' wrote Sir John Glubb (Glubb Pasha of the Arab Legion) in 1967. And again, 'The Moslem World has long been our friend and is closely associated with us.' Since history shows that it is patently not true that the Moslem world has been 'our friend' and since the association has so often been marred by armed conflict it must be assumed that Sir John is speaking subjectively from the very sincerity of his own love and sympathy with individual Arabs, including his own officers and men of the Arab Legion.

When Sir Charles Duke was elected chairman of the Anglo-Arab Association in 1970 he wrote in *The Arab World* (published in London), 'In these difficult times the work of the Anglo-Arab Association of building up understanding and sympathy between people in Great Britain and the Arab countries becomes all the more necessary and important.' The word crops up indirectly. For instance, the pro-Arab publication *Middle East International*, giving biographical details of one of its contributors (April 1971), the distinguished Arabophile, John Reddaway, notes that he is 'a man of wide sympathies, regarded as an authority on Middle East matters'.

But even the most ardent of Arabophiles has difficulty in coming to terms with the ambivalences of the Arab personality. This was shown unwittingly but all the more convincingly by Professor Arnold Toynbee in a letter of July 3, 1967, to an Israeli professor of history. Describing himself as a 'Western spokesman for the Arab cause', Toynbee stated that he felt a responsibility for helping to achieve a permanent peace. 'It is just possible,' he wrote, 'the what I say in public now might have some influence in the Arab world, though it is perhaps more likely that the Arabs might write me off with the verdict that I am no friend of theirs after all.' This was meant as an aside; in fact, Toynbee was expressing a major dilemma felt by so many Westerners when dealing with Arabs. A genuine lover of Arabs, he knew that any sign of compromise or adverse criticism in what he wrote would be taken as betrayal of the 'Arab cause'.

The objective observer is often frustrated by the constant reference to the 'cause' made by people who support the Arabs. It often seems to be the basis of their friendship. But why must there always *be* a cause? These Arabophiles mean, presumably, the Arab cause *vis-à-vis* oil or territory. Would it not be more helpful to the Arabs to talk about the 'inter-Arab dilemma', the 'Arab-world tragedy' or 'the problems of the Arabs'. To speak of 'the Arab cause' implies a conflict, a taking of sides. This is no way to help the Arabs since it only enlarges the gulf between them and the rest of the world. Aware that Arabs are so much their own worst enemies some Englishmen have been quick with their sympathy for the desert dwellers. In 1862–4 W. R. Palgrave, one of several intrepid English travellers who journeyed in Arabia during the nineteenth century, had experiences which led him to find qualities which he believed were shared by Englishmen and by Arabs.

'A strong love and a high appreciation of national and personal liberty, a hatred of minute interference and special regulations, a great respect for authority so long as it be decently well exercised, joined with a remarkable freedom from anything like caste-feeling in what concerns ruling families and dynasties; much practical good sense, much love of commercial enterprise, a great readiness to undertake long journeys by land and sea in search of gain and power; patience to endure, and perseverance in the employment of means to ends, courage in war, vigour in peace, and lastly the marked predominance of a superior race over whomever they come in contact . . . all these are features hardly less characteristic of the Englishman than the Arab.'

134

A modern editor of Palgrave's literary work, Robin Fedden, says that Palgrave was right to sense an affinity between Arabs and Englishmen. 'In spite of profound differences in faith and background, mutual respect and understanding have come easily to both.'*

Foreigners who have lived in some parts of the Arab world have found the children likeable, though more particularly within the discipline of a family or school. The foreign teacher who accepts an appointment in an Arab country finds his charges so under-privileged and under-endowed compared with those he knew in his homeland that he extends to them a natural sympathy. The diplomat, meeting Arabs from good families who are endeavouring to impress him, develops a rapport with them. Few people can make a guest feel more important than upper-class educated Arabs. It is flattering to have one's hands rinsed by the host before or during a meal and to bask in his almost tangible admiration. The Arab is impressed by fame or skill and will lavish attention on anyone with a title or any qualification.

I have good reason to like the first Arabs I knew really well: a wandering desert tribe. In 1956, while gathering material for a book on the battlefields of the 1940–3 North African Campaign I was staying in Tobruk and from here I set out one day to examine the old perimeter lines. I had been ill and had not convalesced long enough. The heat and my exertions that day were too much for me and somewhere out in the sand I collapsed. I woke up in a Bedouin tent where I was gently and courteously treated for several days before the men of the tribe made contact with the British Army base at Tobruk which sent a jeep for me.

During my stay I saw nothing of the women except their eyes—and those at a distance—but their sympathy was evident. Anyway, they could hardly have been more considerate than the men. I was so weak they had to help me drink, urinate and

* *English Travellers in the Near East*, ed. Robin Fedden, The British Council, 1958.

defecate. When they saw I was uncomfortably hot they fanned me but mostly they sensibly let me sleep. It seems almost uncharitable to recall that the tent had a foul smell and that I was covered in flea bites; neither mattered at the time. I had two feelings—gratitude which is still strong, and a pity which I now know was misplaced. Envy of 'total freedom' might have been more appropriate, except that even the Bedouin does not have total freedom. Physically, his movements are restricted to the availability of water; in attitudes he is rigidly bound by centuries of custom—the Arab 'sixth sense'.

Since then I have become friendly with many Arabs of different nations and have tried to maintain a correspondence with them. It always begins well but few Arabs can sustain the effort or interest. The flowery letters deteriorate to brief notes and then silence—though one Libyan sends me his calling card without a word written on it, twice a year.

Probably all Westerners who have lived in an Arab country absorb something from the sun and sand and wind, from the vitality of the bazaars, the grace of traditional Arab dress, the dignity of the minarets and the cool peace of the courtyards, and from the hypnotic droning of Arab music. All this is sensually satisfying and colours the foreigner's vision of the Arab himself. He absorbs a mystique that, in the end, produces the 'violent pro-Arabism'.

A study of the writing and speech of Arabophiles reveals yet another interesting fact—that while it all expresses a well-meant sympathy for the Arabs it draws two quite different pictures. One is a caricature of a humourless, sententious and tediously strident person; the other is a portrait in oils of the 'noble savage' type of desert nomad.

But both are false and to penetrate beyond the caricature and the portrait it is vital to analyse what the Arabs say about themselves.

Discontented with centuries of stagnation, humiliated at having to adopt (until the 1950s) the ways of their conquerors, frustrated in their efforts to wrest more power to direct their own affairs, the Arabs display the combined effect of wounded pride, self-exaltation and self-condemnation. It is the former side that the West sees most often, because that is the side the Arabs present to others. But what the Arab says to the West is much less important than what he says or writes for other Arabs, or what he says when off guard.

Generalizations are safer with Arabs than with most other races because of the unifying traits they themselves emphasize —their devotion to Islam, the Arabic language and Arabic culture. Regional, class sub-cultural and individual differences exist—for instance, the urban Egyptian has a sense of humour and fun that probably no other Arab possesses—but they are no more than group idiosyncrasies.

Psychologically, any comment by an individual is significant in assessing his character and personality. His statements are not necessarily true but sometimes the falsities are more revealing. When they *are* true the manner in which they are framed is often more telling than the truth they express. A man's statements often indirectly disclose boastfulness, self-deception, pride, humility, doubt, anger, inferiority—and much else. Because language is so important to Arabs and because they use so much more of it than many other races it is vividly revealing. In this chapter all but two of the quoted comments are by Arabs about Arabs, but a mere catalogue of comment would be worthless without analysis. For instance, even strongly adverse criticisms cannot necessarily be taken at face value, for an Arab speaks for effect. No two Arabs in conversation can accept the dialogue at face value; each is asking himself 'Why has he said this to me? What does he hope to gain? Is he paying me a compliment because he wants to ask me a favour?'

This internal monologue is constant. So just as Arabs assess the value of utterances so must the foreign analyst.

One aspect of Arab comment on Arabs is more obvious than others—their conspicuous self-glorification. All nations tend to be satisfied with themselves, their virtues and what they regard as their 'mission', even when to other people they are grossly decadent and failing. The Fascists were extolling Italian virtues in 1944 when most of the world no longer had any doubt about the evil which had corrupted the nation.

A study of what Arabs say—and do not say—will no doubt become a major part of university courses on 'Arab Studies'. The contrast with other nations is startling. For instance, Arab spokesmen habitually address their hearers as members of a proud and noble people (*nabīl, karīm, abī*). The Egyptian Mahmud Na'na'a speaks of '. . . the battle for life through which our glorious Arab nation is living with heroism, manliness, and endurance.' In official announcements, which in most countries are couched in unemotional terms, we find, for example: 'Our valiant armies and our valiant pilots. . . .'

When the Egyptian Army went to war in October 1973, the Chief of Staff, General Shazli, began his order of the day: 'My sons, officers and men. Sons of Egypt, best soldiers on earth, scions of the great Pharaohs, sons of the intrepid Arabs!'

Mohammad Al-Qusrī, a Syrian, in a play called *Palestine, the Tragedy of the Arab World*, says of the Arabs: 'There is none among the nations of the entire world so good as the Arabs, and they are a noble people.' In another place he defines them as '. . . a proud people which injustice does not allow to sleep, which speedily takes vengeance and regards hatred for its enemies as a duty rather than a necessity.'

Darwish al-Jundi, an Egyptian, says that the Arab is undoubtedly different from Europeans and Far Easterners since historically his life has given him 'certain traditions and a particular view of virtue and goodness'. The Arab is courageous but despite his great courage in war, he is very humane. He is generous, enlightened, tolerant, faithful to his promise, averse to all illusions and superstition, and protects the weak. He is eloquent and is enchanted by sublime literature.*

The Professor of the Faculty of Arts at Cairo University, Dr Ibrahim Juma'a, goes much further. He told me in 1956 that

* *Arab Nationalism in Modern Arab Literature*, 1962.

'the genuine Arab code of morality, graced and systematized by a divine message, restored dignity to mankind'.* The extravagance and historical inaccuracy of what followed accounts for my noting it so fully at the time. This Arab code, Dr Juma'a said, 'converted injustice to justice, fear into tranquillity, war into peace, and slavery into freedom. It reconciled the followers of Mohammad with the followers of Christ, declared all men free and equal, and established democracy, socialism and a co-operative spirit long before these systems of life had been regulated and codified elsewhere.' The Arabs, he claimed, were the guides and counsellors of mankind since they were the first to define national conduct and the first to originate a human ideology which they then implemented and made into a code of ethics for mankind.

In his book, Dr Juma'a goes further with his adulation than he did when speaking to me and, like so many Arab intellectuals, he presents the ideal as if it were the norm. In the Arab world, he states, there is no trace of monopoly, opportunism and exploitation. Production develops according to scientific methods, equality of opportunity is assured and just distribution of income is guaranteed. This is starkly in contradiction of the facts in Egypt of 1960, where the fellaheen were blatantly exploited by the rich landowners, where 'scientific method' was virtually non-existent, where opportunities did not exist for 90 per cent of the population and 'just distribution of income' kept the majority at starvation level.

'The Arabs have always been unique in their firmness and moderation; God himself so disposed them,' Juma'a asserts, though on the same page of his book is a footnote about Abdallah ibn al-Muqaffa, 'put to death about the year 757 because his orthodoxy was suspect'.

H. H. Ayrout, an Egyptian author, has written more realistically about his own people and shows compassion for the fellaheen, whose poverty and oppression for thousands of years

* He later used all these thoughts in his *Ideology of Arab Nationalism in Emergence from the Consciousness of the Arabs*, Cairo, 1960.

have given them a passive and docile, though cunning, mentality. 'Resignation is scarcely strong enough to describe the degradation imposed on the fellaheen. . . . The fellah acts like a child or a brute because he is treated like one. It is said that the fellaheen cannot understand an authority that is humane and appeals to their better instincts. . . . The reason is that they have been brought up to nothing but blows, fines, insults and bullying. . . . Nobody has done anything to teach the fellah . . . qualities or to give him moral encouragement.'*

Ayrout's frankness is not characteristic. The more usual self-glorification may be a compensation for the dissatisfaction and frustration caused by the position of the Arabs in the world—achievement of satisfaction by the enhancement of one's own value through images and daydreams of grandeur. Arab writers often emphasize their contribution to culture, especially in reaction to Western criticism. Abd al-Latif Sharāra declares, for instance, in reply to Bertrand Russell's slighting view of the original Arab contribution to philosophy, ' "Man" is the greatest invention in the world, which was discovered by Arab culture.'

Also, 'The Arabs are more interested than any other people in humanist studies, especially history, geography, legislation, language, ethics and medicine.' Some Arab writers claim that their race was the first to make important discoveries and inventions. Mahmud Rousan, an Egyptian, declares, 'The Arab invented the wheel, on which modern civilization is built, and is now supplying the oil to keep that wheel turning.'

Arab writers frequently sing the praises of Arab nationalism. Unlike other forms of nationalism, which are merely a transitional stage, Arab nationalism is 'eternal', as the Ba'ath constitution declares, and 'has an eternal mission to mankind'. Dr Abdal-Bazzaz, like other ideologists, enumerates the essential qualities: it is universal, democratic, Arab-Socialist, progressive, revolutionary, positive and active. All these characteristics are inseparable parts of its very being. The concept of '*Uruba*

* *The Fellaheen*, Cairo, 1945.

(Arabism) is so heavily loaded with adoration, that Arabs appear to distinguish between it as an abstract entity, which exists apart from its bearers, and the Arabs themselves. Arabism is greater and more sublime than its embodiment in the Arabs, but, on the other hand, the sublimity of Arabism is believed to be a guarantee that the Arabs will be worthy of it.

Another interesting aspect of the Arab mind is near-obsession with criticism, cogently expressed by Dr Fayez Sayegh, formerly an Arab spokesman at the United Nations. Writing in 1953, Dr Sayegh says, 'The Arab is fascinated with criticism—of foreigners, of fellow countrymen, of leaders, of followers— always of "the other", seldom of oneself—which is the product of basic dissatisfaction and general discontent rather than of positive convictions and allegiances and standards, and which accordingly serves to thwart collective personal accomplishment rather than to stimulate creative effort and bold enterprise.'

Self-criticism is usually directed against some kind of failure, rather than against an attitude which could have led to failure. A typical example of self-criticism about approach rather than attitude is an article, 'The Arabs, Their Own Enemies', in the Beirut daily *Al-Hayat*, June 24, 1959.

'The entire Arab mentality is in need of a fundamental transformation. . . . Since . . . the second decade of this century, the Arabs have known nothing but negation. . . . We demand what we want, but we do not think about what we are capable of doing, and thus we achieved nothing. . . .

'Events [in Palestine] have developed in opposition to our aspirations. We did not demand or act in accordance with our capacity and we were not content with the possible. Thus we have been living for over a third of a century in illusionary hopes, hopes devoid of logic and practicability, will and loyalty, entranced by the deceptive spell of falsehood and ignorance.

'When will we have a practical policy, based on **Arab,**

141

regional and international facts? The whole world laughs at the Arabs. . . . And what will history say? The Arabs were victims of themselves, their ignorance, their blindness and their arrogance.

'O God, be lenient to us and pardon us! O God, give us wisdom, even before nobility, honour, exaltation, glory and the righteous road.

'O God, shorten our tongues and broaden our logic.'

But the logic in studies of Arab history being written today in Arab countries is seriously criticized by orientalists. Von Grunebaum notes the influence of the Arabs' self-image on the writing of their history. Because of their dissatisfaction with the position in the present, the Arabs seek encouragement in the past, where they find the glory which they lack today. In this quest they are selective. They tend to choose a number of episodes in the past, which show success, and use them to cover up failures of which they are not particularly proud. History assumes an apologetic character. Professor Cantwell Smith, of Harvard University, believes that 'The Arab writing of history has been functioning less as a genuine inquiry than as a psychological defence. Most of it is to be explained primarily in terms of the emotional needs that it fulfils.'*

Dr Sayegh has made one of the frankest assessments of the Arab's emotional inadequacies.† He refers to 'The Arab's apparent incapacity for disciplined and abiding unity, his self-centredness, manifesting itself into chaos and disorganization, his reluctance to assume responsibility for his personal and national misfortunes, and his inclination to put the entire blame upon the shoulders of 'others', his impatience, his lack of steady perseverance and unyielding persistence in the pursuit of objectives which is but an echo of half-heartedness of his faith in those objectives or in himself. . . .'

* *Islam in Modern History*, Princeton University Press, 1957.
† Probably written in 1953 but given to me by Dr Sayegh in Beirut, January 1972.

Inadequacies of another kind were identified by Ishaq Musa al-Husayni, a Palestinian living in Cairo, in a 1954 article on the causes of crises in Arab thought.* He listed them as:

Uncertainty. Because of widespread faith in destiny, there is little planning.

Extemporization. When problems arise suddenly, solutions are improvised that are often wrong.

Absence of reason, of correct and logical thinking based on study and meditation. 'We have no writers researching and studying our various problems, recording their opinions and transmitting their knowledge to successors in order to evolve a scholarly heritage embracing all walks of life.'

Absence of courage, ideological freedom and self-criticism. 'The thinking man among us is suspect. If he departs from the ordinary, he is accused of hypocrisy or unbelief. Thus, freedom of thought is imprisoned within us, where it tortures our conscience, and the crisis becomes worse from one generation to the next. The modern life enjoyed by other men is an object of envy for us when we visit the West.

Obsession with the past. This, al-Husayni states, paralyses the Arab mind.

A more recent assessment of the Arab personality is that of Dr Sadiq Jalal al'Azm who describes the Arab as a person in search of short-cuts in place of hard work and maximum effort to reach the desired goal, with sudden enthusiasms, foolhardiness and, since he underestimates obstacles, with quickly receding interest. The author attributes to this 'Fahlawi personality'—the West would call it Le Grand Seigneur personality—a burning preoccupation with surface impression. The Arab, he says, is not interested in true, workmanlike accomplishment that comes only through hard and systematic work, but rather in avoiding the impression that he is incapable of accomplishing things. Such a person cannot admit failure; he wants to masquerade as a success, and finally always looks for some

* Beirut, 1954.

Koran condemn Arab.

scapegoat to cover up his lack of accomplishment, whether in politics or battle.*

Following his comments, Dr al'Azm was charged, in Lebanon, with having criticized Islam and having fomented discord among religious factions. In July 1970 the Court of Appeals quashed the conviction and commended him for having asked in his book whether Moslems of the twentieth century must believe the literal truth of the Koranic stories. This a doctrine Br

The always-frank Albert Hourani concedes that Arabs have a 'psychological weakness'. He reasons that because they refuse to recognize a distasteful situation they are unable to define their relationship to that situation and cannot distinguish between what they would like ideally and what they are capable of achieving in practice. Arabs, he says, have a great capacity for self-deception and moral cowardice.

This self-deception has produced much Arab political literature which castigates Arabs for failure to live in a world of reality. King Abdullah of Jordan was unequivocal about it. 'Arabs must give up daydreaming and apply themselves to realities.'† The Jordanian White Paper of 1967 is even more severe. 'If we Arabs do not leave behind the reasons for our weakness, then our living in the world of dreams will almost certainly reduce us to the lowest level or to the disappearance of the nation.'

Mohammad Haikal, writing in *Al-Ahram*, January 1964, criticized the Arabs for being afraid to employ their power. 'We have tremendous, unlimited strength at our disposal in the political, economic and military fields, but our hands tremble even before we start to employ it. Why? Because we do not possess a realistic estimate of this strength. Its utilization is, therefore, an adventure into the unknown.'

Sania Hamady, like Haikal, believes that the Arab has a 'high-level of potential intelligence and remarkable native intelligence' but notes that he has practically no ability to gener-

* *Self-Criticism After the Defeat*, Beirut, 1968.
† *My Memoirs Completed*, Amman, 1951.

alize or to grasp the whole of any concept. Dr Jamil Saliba, a leading educator from Damascus, agrees that the Arab cannot comprehend any plan or concept in its entirety and emphasizes that while the Syrians and Lebanese are extreme individualists they want their government to do everything for them. 'They ask their governments to plant their deserts with figs and olives, to make their wells gush forth, to revive the land for them, and to guarantee their livelihood. But whenever they are called upon to work in co-operation, they object and each one prefers to do the work individually.' Saliba regrets that the Arab cannot conceive that various interests can be harmonized in such a way as to make a general rule work in his own interest. He will not be bound by any system imposed from outside. His main concern is with his private welfare and since this applies to nearly all Arabs any system imposed from outside is inevitably chaotic because it must be composed of the incompatible inclinations, desires and interests of individuals.

These incompatibilities and individualistic interests have been obstacles for those psychologists who have carried out personality studies among Arabs. Dr Shakir Ammar, an Egyptian, analysed people from his own village but still found reserve, suspicion and constriction. 'Hearty laughter is rare, and it usually occurs among adults in their sarcastic allusions to others, and in belittling their esteem, while apparently seeming to praise them. Suspicion of the evil intentions of others is institutionalized in the evil eye, seeing potential danger in practically everybody. . . . The almost morbid fear of shame, the excessive touchiness, the frequent resort to the use of oaths and swearing, the exaggerated expressions of language, are all symptoms of a type of personal relationship which could not be legitimately described as intimate and smooth.'

Ammar explains behaviour on the basis of child-rearing methods. Besides physical punishment and ridicule, another way of enforcing conformity is through the use of fear of imaginary creatures. The 'ghoul' is often described as an imaginary beast with a huge and hairy body who devours

145

wicked children. Ammar recalls that many of the children of the village were certain that they had actually seen 'ghouls'. During these early years, the child is made to fear and show respect to certain 'sacred' objects, which ultimately develop into a complex world of superstitious practices. To evade punishment, the child develops a knack for telling lies; Ammar says, 'The effects of techniques of fear such as forcing children to resort to lies and deception, are reflected later in the prevailing atmosphere of *adult life which is charged with suspicion, secrecy and apprehension.*'

This might appear to indicate that Arab society is under-developed. The real truth could be that it is, in a particular way, over-developed. As I have tried to show, Arab culture of the past was not primitive; it had a rare depth and finesse. Probably it was finer than our own Western culture, of whatever political colour. In effect, Arab culture became over-ripe and the effects can be seen in speech and imagination, in the front the Arab presents to the world and in the complexity of his make-up. Hence suspicion, secrecy and apprehension, while innate, are taken to extremes in the great difficulties of coming to terms with a world that has outstripped Arab society.

I once spent several weeks in Tripoli, Libya, seeking an interview with President Qaddhafi and the preliminaries imposed on me illustrated suspicion, secrecy and apprehension, all three. Various presidential aides cross-examined me. Was I a Jew? Not even part-Jew? Who had suggested that I write about President Qaddhafi? What would I write? Could I guarantee that the report would be favourable?

Appointments were made and cancelled or a car which was supposed to call for me simply did not arrive. To show good faith I sent the President copies of two of my books and that brought another round of questions. Why had I sent the books? Why these particular books? Why had I written my name in the books? The anguish of the officials delegated to deal with me was considerable since nobody wanted to take the responsibility of granting the interview. All these officials later signed documents that they had given me no 'confidential information'. A senior officer of the Ministry of Information showed me the files kept on virtually every non-Arab journalist who had written on any Arab subject for the Press. Many were no longer welcome in Libya because they had been critical. And this was the main difficulty about me: the Libyans had records of me as an author of books but no cuttings of anything I had written for newspapers. 'I can tell you certain things about the President,' this officer said, 'but all of it must be kept secret.'

Those Arabs who have spent long years in the West or have emigrated there see their countries with sympathy and perspective. Abdul Aziz Said, a Syrian who grew up in the province of al-Jazirah, was a 'revolutionary' from the age of thirteen. He confesses that he equated demonstration with revolution and, finally, disillusioned by the constant military coups and by military government he went to the United States, where he teaches political science. He would like to see a revolution—by which he means a process of significant change—but considers this unlikely. He says, 'The Arab remains comfortable with his identity, making it difficult for him to entertain revolutionary ideas. Even when he does, he wages his revolution on the battlefield of rhetoric.* In a region where there have always been appropriate audiences and garrulous orators, the faces are the same; only the masks are new. . . . Leaders have [merely] affected revolutionary postures. In the Arab world revolution

* An example of rhetoric: 'Leap ahead, our brave soldiers, to complete your mission . . . the liberation of every grain of sand defiled by the enemy's feet, regardless of the efforts and sacrifices, and regardless of how long the battle may continue. Fulfil the hopes of Egypt and the Arab nation. Know that you are not alone in your fight. Everyone is anxious to fight on your side, because your victories in this campaign will put an end to the imperialist plans directed against all the nations of the region. Remain confident that every drop of blood lost in the battlefield will be preceded by a torrent of blood from our enemies and the enemies of Allah.' Egypt's Minister of War, General Ismail Ali, addressing the armed forces of Egypt and Syria (Middle East News Agency, Cairo, October 11, 1973).

is merely a medium, . . . a justification for the rivalry of pretenders for power.'*

There are hints here about the inflated personality and ostentatiousness of the Arab, which many Arab observers concede. It is partly the result of the language which readily lends itself to assertion and exaggeration. Probably allied to this is the feeling that any regulation may be circumvented—and it usually can be. Many times blocked by officialdom in my journalistic work, I have asked Arab friends for help; I cannot recall a single case in which the friend himself could solve my problem, but he had a brother or a cousin or an uncle who could do so—and did. Invariably the exercise gave them great satisfaction.

A Palestinian psychologist, a graduate of the American University of Beirut, once told me to remember, in any discussion with an Arab, that he would be hiding something—such as unhappiness or ignorance, his poverty or his pleasure. 'He will only be half listening to you because his centre of gravity is internal; he is too preoccupied with self to concentrate on you.'

Collectively, Arab observers of Arabs make similar points. The Arab, they say, is often so busy advancing services and goods to various members of his group and collecting from them in return that he has little time for discussion with foreigners. Strangers should not expect demonstrations of joy; the more a person controls his gaiety the more he is respected. Acute awareness of dignity prevents most Arabs from any display of 'frivolity', so laughter is rare. Again, the Arab is a sad person—a generalization valid in every Arab country if not necessarily in every group. He is pessimistic, perhaps because death, impermanence and the cheapness of things are always on his mind.

While few Arab students of Arab behaviour so claim, it is a fact that many Arabs have great charm and excellent manners. On first contact the Arab is gentle, courteous, generous and usually ready to oblige; indeed, he will promise much more

* 'Arabs and Revolution,' an essay in *People and Politics in the Middle East*, New York, 1971.

than he can possibly fulfil. Arabs—women as much as men in emancipated groups—are masters of the compliment and of flattery.

If there is one aspect of the Arab personality on which most observers agree it is that the Arab is not yet really an individual, not a person. His personality has been stunted by his dependence on his family. Not yet weaned from it, he has no self-reliance and he cannot solve his own problems. Nor can he think for himself or use his initiative. Independence of mind has no particular virtue.

The Westerner involved in negotiations with Arabs must begin with certain basic assumptions, and possibly Sania Hamady is the best authority for them. She stresses that the Arab gives because he expects to receive; that he is tied hand and foot by the demands and interferences of his group; that the Arab becomes enthusiastic and proclaims his readiness to act but when the time comes for action he shies away, and that he feels debased if he is pitied. It is Hamady, too, who draws attention to the Arab's quick, intense anger. The slightest provocation antagonizes him and his wrath has no limits. Enraged, he attacks others and will take advantage of them. Again the Arab is inclined to judge a person by a single trait and from a chance and insignificant remark he is likely to draw extreme conclusions and to pass them on, for gossip is endemic in Arab society. Finally, and perhaps most importantly, no foreigner should assume that because an Arab does not say 'no' that he means 'yes'. Almost every Arab will avoid a blunt refusal, largely because it is improper to rebuff people so brusquely. Those Westerners who assume an affirmative in the absence of a negative and then condemn the Arab when they find they are wrong, are doing the Arab an injustice; he does not intend to deceive, even when he lies to avoid the responsibility of saying no.

The difficulties facing the Westerner dealing with the Arabs are minor in comparison with those which face the young, impatient and intellectual Arabs who want a true revolution—one

149

of changing attitudes and values—in the Arab world. Ramadan Lawand, a young Lebanese intellectual, speaks for many when he says, 'We want a new leadership which can end this crisis that has plagued us and perverted our values. We want this leadership to steer us back to the path laid down by life's youthful urge. We desire a dignified nation whose humanism is apparent in all its politics, thought and feelings.'

'Life's youthful urge' is Lawand's key phrase; his revolution has already begun when an Arab values that period between birth and death more highly than the past or the unknown but pre-destined (Islamic) future.

Since this chapter began with comments by foreigners, it might be appropriate to conclude with an observation by Professor Larry Hochman, of the University of Eastern Michigan. Writing in *The Arab World*, New York, June 1969, he said that 'The emancipation of the Arab people must be the act of the Arab people themselves, country by country. That is the primary revolutionary task and the fruits of that revolution can be productivization, liberation, democratization, self-determination and justice.'

Unequivocal in his liking for the Arabs, Professor Hochman did not find it necessary to patronize them by expressing 'sympathy' for them.

9 *Rule by Army Officers*

self defense

In Islam you kill only in self defense according to Quran. 4:92, 93, 94

'The Arabs fear and respect rank; this is why Army officers must govern the Arab lands.' President (Colonel) Nasser to the author, Cairo, 1956.

'Who else but Army officers are in a position to lead the Arab revolution?' Prime Minister (Major) Abdel Jalloud of Libya to the author, Tripoli, 1972.

'He who is the enemy of my enemy is my friend.' Arab proverb.

Nothing has had a more profound effect on the Arab mind—not even obsession with Israel—than the rise to power of Army officers in the Arab states. This phenomenon coincides with a world trend towards renewed militarism which could easily obscure the real reasons for Arab officer-rule and it is necessary to understand that military coups in the Arab world are rooted in racial history and are the heritage of Islamic civilization.

Islam is a belligerent and militaristic ideology. This is not denigratory but a fact borne out by exhortations in the Koran and in every work based on the Koran. Nothing in Islamic writing recurs more frequently than the principle of holy war, a religious duty obligatory on the community of believers.

Holy War has to be inside you killing you ego

'. . . How many a city We have destroyed! Our might came upon it at night, or while they enjoyed their ease at noontide.' Sura vii: 'The Battlements'.

'. . . When you encounter the unbelievers marching to battle, do not turn your backs on them. . . . Fight them until . . . the religion is Allah's entirely.' Sura viii: 'The Spoils'.

'Oh Prophet [Allah is speaking to Mohammad], urge on the

151

believers to fight. If there be twenty of you . . . they will overcome two hundred. . . . It is not for any Prophet to take prisoners until he make wide slaughter in the land.' Ibid.

In recent generations, when Islam was no longer on the offensive, attacking and expanding, but on the defensive, the concept of jihad was sometimes given a new apologetic interpretation of a moral struggle against the individual's evil inclinations and of the people's aspirations for social reforms, but the original meaning of the principle has never disappeared. The Moslem Brotherhood advocate a jihad to establish a fanatical, aggressive Islamic regime. In April 1953 Anwar Sadat proclaimed in a Cairo mosque, 'The jihad is a religious duty of all Moslems,' and he was not referring specifically to action against Israel.

Obviously, in a society which has been taught that war and conflict is as necessary as it is inevitable, great status falls on the military leaders whose function it will be to wage the jihad. The ordinary people, by their mental conditioning over many centuries, are inclined to accept this military overlordship. They have been accustomed to the sight of uniforms and arms and the exercise of force through a tradition of conquests and the regimes of military usurpers and conquerors. The Arab writer George M. Haddad calls this ceaseless oppression 'the burden of history in the Middle East'.

The military burden can be oppressive, as in Syria's case. This is the resumé of coups:

Colonel Husni Za'im.	Successful in March 1949. Executed in August 1949.
Colonel Sami Hinnawi.	Successful in 1949. Murdered in 1950.
Colonel Adib Shishakli.	Successful in 1950. Murdered (in Brazil) in 1964.
Colonel Louay Atassi.	Successful in 1963. Ousted in the same year.

General Amin al-Hafez.	Successful in 1963.
	Arrested and exiled in 1966.
Major-General Salah Jedid.	Successful in 1966.
	Ousted and arrested in 1970.

In every Arab country one finds Service officers involved in plots and coups to a much greater extent than the intellectuals or straightforward political opportunists who engineer most coups in other countries.

The motives behind the officers' activities are only partly based on the age-old fixation with jihad. Other forces are at work, though they are at times confused. For instance, Arab officer politicians label themselves as 'nationalist revolutionary' or 'revolutionary nationalist'. The contradiction implicit in these terms illustrates the difficulties of analysing their role. The officers themselves define it as that of 'intelligentsia in uniform' while middle-class civilians see them as 'the armed intelligentsia'. Confusion apart, at least there seems to be some awareness in these labels of the high status of the officers and it gives a clear idea of their self-image.

Unfortunately, the expression *muthaqqaf* (intellectual) has become so abused in modern Arabic that its original meaning is blurred. In the Arab world anyone who knows how to read and write and does not engage in manual labour is an intellectual, just as every teacher, clerk and official is one. It is part of the distortion of values by which a pupils' riot becomes a 'students' demonstration'. Formerly, the term *muthaqqaf* was used discriminatingly, as intellectual still is in Western languages, and did not apply as a blanket description to everybody with some learning.

It is true that Army officers are educated but few would be classed as intellectuals in the Western sense, for the very reason that few officers in Western armies are intellectuals; they are Establishment figures and the very nature of their training tends to make them unquestioning and less flexible. The officer class is a defined and closed professional and social group, relatively

153

separated from the rest of society; in Arab countries it has a highly fostered group consciousness and superiority.

As early as 1931 the role of the officer class among the Arab intelligentsia and the nationalist-conscious elements was exaggerated. Social and ideological developments have broadened and diversified the ranks of the educated, and the officer class can no longer claim to have a monopoly of the characteristics of the intelligentsia. However, the idealization of the officer class as the perfect and almost exclusive representative of the intelligentsia persists—and not only among those who themselves wear uniform. In a discussion among Soviet experts in 1964 on the subject of 'Socialism, Capitalism and the under-developed countries', G. Mirskiy said that in those countries the officers are 'the best-educated section of the intelligentsia, always better equipped than others with progressive ideologies' and they 'struggle for the modernization of their backward countries'.*

Mirskiy revised his statement when he dealt, in 1967, with the problem of 'the army and politics in the third world'. Then he wrote: 'The ideological outlook of the military leaders is bourgeois in respect to its background and remains today the principal support of neo-colonialism. They [the military dictators in different countries of Asia, Africa and Latin America] have no taste for large-scale social changes. They also lack the necessary qualifications for leadership of a state.'†

In the Arab countries, as elsewhere in Asia and Africa, other groups of intellectuals are superior to the officer class in education and more advanced in political and social mentality and ideas. The officer class can now claim precedence in power alone.

In their drive for power Arab officers are sometimes inspired by the best of motives. Colonel Naguib, in deposing King

* G. Mirskiy, 'Creative Marxism and problems of national liberation revolution', *Mirovaya Ekonomika: Mezhdunarodnyye Otnosheniya*, No. 5, 1963, translated in the *Mizan Newsletter*, No. 7, London, April 1964.

† G. Mirskiy, 'The army and politics in the third world,' *Literaturnaya gazeta*, No. 32, Moscow, August 2, 1967.

Farouk in 1952, was expressing a distaste for regal corruption and national moral bankruptcy but he was ill-equipped to cure the country's ills. Nasser, who deposed Naguib, was little better fitted for the task but even a slight achievement in a country as backward as Egypt in the early 1950s was a major success. Nasser's personal magnetism and confidence gave the Egyptians and ultimately all Arabs the feeling that here was a successor to the Prophet. Yet Nasser told me, in April 1956, 'The British will have to go but I wish, personally, that they could stay. Whatever their faults the British produce a sense of security. And we Egyptians are an insecure people.'*

One point perhaps not fully appreciated in the West is that Arab military coups are *officer* coups and exclusively so. The troops are always readily moulded for it is axiomatic that the Arab soldier obeys his commander blindly, whoever the enemy, even when the commander is guilty of extreme disobedience to those to whom he has sworn allegiance. There is no evidence that Arab soldiers have been asked for their opinions or even that they have been deemed to possess opinions. Only rarely has an officer thought it necessary to give any explanation to his soldiers and when he has done so it has been to overcome hesitancy. For instance, in September 1961 an Egyptian major serving in Syria was faced with a revolt of people wishing to secede from the United Arab Republic—that is, the union of Syria and Egypt. He wanted to move a brigade of men from Qutaifa to Damascus and told his Syrian troops, who were surprised by the sudden command, that they were travelling to repel an 'Israeli surprise attack'. Since the revolt was a national Syrian rising against Egypt the major was taking a big risk, especially as he did not have the authority of his brigade commander—a Syrian.

Among the principal Arab officer-politicians attitudes to Islam differ. There are the fanatics, such as Abd al-Salaam Aref,

---

* He also told me that a brigade of Australian troops could hold Egypt while divisions of British could never do it. 'The Australians smile when they beat you up.'

the Iraqi who murdered his former colleague, Qassem; and Qaddhafi of Libya; the moderates, such as Naguib; the religiously indifferent, of whom Qassem is a prime example, and the reformers, such as Husni Za'im of Syria, the instigator and then the victim of separate coups. Nasser, though a devout Moslem, appeared to want to neutralize religion as a political force but he was still approaching this with extreme caution at the time of his death. No Arab officer-politician has moved along the path of secularization taken by Kemal Ataturk in Turkey. Most are trapped by a dichotomy—they want to free themselves from the rule of Islam as a dogma but all are chained to Islam as a community. And since Islam is a religious community it is virtually impossible for the officers to cut away the dogma.

Still, when they achieved political power, many officers took steps which conflicted with tradition; they granted suffrage to women, for instance. Qassem and Nasser had women cabinet ministers. In Egypt the religious courts for adjudicating laws of personal status were abolished. But these and similar measures are the continuation of a development which began long before the officers reached power and it would have progressed without them. Similar progress has been achieved in Arab countries without officer governments; in Tunisia, President Bourguiba brought about a radical separation of church and state and, significantly, officers have less influence there than in any other Arab land. In February 1960 Bourguiba took the genuinely revolutionary step of demanding that the religious leaders should allow workmen to eat during working hours in the fasting month of Ramadan.

Arab officer-politicians, and notably the 'Free Officers' responsible for the Egyptian coup of 1952, always insisted that the officers came from the 'masses of the people'—a claim by Naguib. This should be examined. Most Egyptian officers at that time were sons and brothers of officials, army and police officers and middle-class members of the professions; some came from well-to-do farming families. It is true that a few

were related to the couple of hundred families of great landowners, bankers, industrialists and big businessmen. But it is
equally true that *none* of the officers came from the 80 per
cent of the Egyptian populace, that is, the artisans and small
traders, the urban and rural labourers. So they were not really
'of the people'.

Some changes did occur after 1952 but they affected the
position of the officer class more than its composition. The
Free Officers cashiered 420 senior officers—all above the rank
of colonel and most of the colonels. The only exceptions were
Naguib himself and one other. The leaders of the Free Officers,
wanting to devote themselves to politics, promoted to senior
commands those officers they considered 'politically faithful
and professionally qualified'. This assured the loyalty of the
greater number of officers. Nobody was permitted to 'jump'
ranks, as is so frequent in the Syrian army. The only exception
in Egypt was Abd al-Hakim Amir who was promoted from
major to brigadier in 1953, to lieutenant-general in 1957 and to
marshal in 1958. He was largely responsible for the Egyptian
defeat in 1967 and committed suicide—or was murdered.

The gulf between Egyptian officers and men is wide. After
the 1956 Sinai Campaign and the Six-Day War of June 1967
the Israelis, always interested in Arab psychology, held a large
number of officers in one place while they were asked the usual
routine questions. Then, in the presence of some foreign
journalists, they were permitted to make their own requests and
to ask questions. The majority asked for better conditions
for themselves, some asked if officers of their acquaintance
had been captured or wounded, many were interested in the
progress of the conflict. Not a single one asked about his
men.

With few exceptions, officers have abused the power and
privileges produced by politics. Being the rulers, they are able
to seize opportunities for social, economic and political ad-
vancement but only at the expense of intensive lobbying,
rivalry and corruption. The case of Majdi Hasanayn is an

interesting one but not extreme. A major before the revolution of 1952, he was a close friend of Nasser and a member of the Free Officers. He put forward the idea of the 'Liberation Province', a rural area to be treated as a model agricultural and co-operative project. He went to Europe to buy machinery —although he had no technical knowledge—and through his much-publicized project became a leading figure in Egyptian life. In 1956 the scheme was an obvious and costly failure but by then Hasanayn had built himself a magnificent house and was living like an old-type pasha. Public and private pressure forced Nasser to dismiss Hasanayn in 1957 but a year later he was manager of the National Cement Company, importing *sand* from Britain for making local cement. He survived and prospered until 1966 when Nasser got rid of him by making him ambassador to Czechoslovakia.

The make-up of the Iraqi officer corps is different from the Egyptian; several hundred officers come from two backgrounds almost foreign to the Egyptian forces—the privileged and wealthy families and from those of the Moslem clergy. But the largest number of officers are from middle-class urban families, the sons of junior officials and small traders. In all three major groups many officers are related to other officers. This mixture has all the elements for extreme conflict. The wealthy officers find plenty of acolytes among the poorer ones; the sons of the Moslem clergy, often fanatical, demand and get the allegiance of the more religious poorer officers. The cliques which develop support a series of continuous Service feuds.

The Iraqi officer class dominates Iraqi politics with inevitable in-fighting, corruption and cruelty, the latter often directed against other officers. Psychologically this is explicable. Army officers are not usually given to discussion of differences; their training is in command and an order is not the basis of rational debate. So when two officers intent on power confront each other one has to go under and when he does he must be made to 'confess' to his 'plotting' and be punished so that he will not default again. As before, a mere explanation of the situation that he has lost the competition is not considered salutary or lasting enough.

All this is illustrated by a series of events that took place in July 1968. On the 17th of that month Colonel Naef and General Hassan al-Bakr overthrew the government of the Aref regime. On the 30th al-Bakr banished Colonel Naef and then imprisoned and tortured Chief-of-Staff General al-Ansari and two former Prime Ministers because al-Bakr feared that these men planned yet another coup—against him.

The process is continual, and violence is usually arbitrary and sudden. For instance, early in July 1973 the Director of Public Security, Colonel Nazem Kazzar, and thirty-five officers were allegedly involved in a coup against President al-Bakr. Defence Minister Hammad Shebab was killed—by Kazzar personally, it was stated—and another cabinet minister was wounded. But officers loyal to al-Bakr caught Kazzar after a cross-country chase. Within a week he and his fellow conspirators were tried and convicted; within two hours they were shot by firing squad. President al-Bakr announced that others would be shot, 'without trial if necessary'.

The Syrian officer corps is more varied in composition than the Egyptian and Iraqi, with many officers from poor families (though the poorest of the poor in Syria are well off compared with the human beasts of burden in Egypt and Iraq). Others come from distinguished and wealthy families. But the majority are the sons of well-to-do peasant farmers, traders and professional men. This could give the impression that the army is well balanced but it is subjected to more shocks and instability than any Arab army. In fact, it is tense with recurring and sudden changes in command, usually with upheavals that penetrate down to battalion level. Officers are promoted and demoted several ranks at a time and often for no militarily justifiable reason. Frequent transfers, dismissals and purges are unsettling. But even greater stress results from the heavy and insistent indoctrination along Ba'athist party lines. This has the effect of making the Syrian officers arrogant, intellectually

159

introverted and ruthless in support or suppression of a coup. In July 1963 they bloodily put down the Alwan rebellion led by Colonel Jasim Alwan, commander of the Aleppo garrison. The same year, and several times since, they crushed Kurdish risings.

Again, the officers quelled with brutal severity a strike by merchants in Hama in April 1964; this was the only serious movement to shake the government without officers directing its course and it was, therefore, seen as a particular danger.

The influence of the Ba'ath philosophy is pernicious. Mohammad Haikal has said that the Ba'ath's internecine struggles 'recall the quarrels of the Mafia gangs in Sicily and America who join forces for the purpose of taking plunder and then fight each other to the death in dividing the spoils'. It seems probable that nobody in the Middle East speaks so much about unity as the Ba'ath leadership and nobody does so much to deepen conflict and promote discord. In February 1974, for instance, a peace was arranged between the Iraqi army and the Kurds and the whole Arab world was relieved—except for the Ba'athists, the only group to protest against the ceasefire. In inter-Arab relationships Ba'ath officer politicians have become incomparably quarrelsome, while internally they possess the monopoly of institutionalized violence.

A study of the reasons officers give for seizure of political power is interesting. The most significant fact is that they rarely mention anything to do with the army itself—such as greater military efficiency or better social conditions. The officer who assumes control announces that the army has taken over the country to fight corruption, to prevent anarchy, to establish a regime based on freedom and justice, to liberate the country from imperialism and make it economically independent, to advance the cause of Arab unity. Officers are spectacularly ill-fitted to carry out any of these ill-defined tasks, but, with ever-increasing arbitrary rule, they attempt them. The result is further damage to Arab confidence and expression.

Throughout the Arab states officer-politicians perpetuate the idea that they are working for the people and perhaps, having made this statement, they really believe they are doing so; in fact, they are striving for the betterment of their own élite group, while keeping a wary eye on the aspirations of officer sub-groups.

Arab officers generally seem to regard a coup and a revolution as one and the same. In conversation, Qaddhafi repeatedly refers to 'the revolution of September 1'—the 1969 day when he and other officers seized control of the country from King Idris' government. In making the terms synonymous the officer-politicians are psychologically confusing their own people, for the two happenings are significantly different. A coup is a single act while a revolution is a continuous movement. The main feature of a coup is a change of government—but it is only one of the features of a revolution, usually not the first and never the last. A coup is an occurrence, a revolution is an era. Again, while a coup 'happens' the people are like spectators at a play, condemning or approving, applauding, or frowning in disapproval. But in a revolution masses of the people are performers in the play. The Arab officers often genuinely believe, such is their political naïvety, that in executing a coup they have completed the revolution. They have merely made way for it —but then they at once prevent it from developing. This is one of the great ironies of the Arab world—and of other areas where military coups flourish.

In Tripoli in 1972 I was several times invited to attend meetings of young officers planning a rising against Colonel Qaddhafi and his twelve-man Revolutionary Command Council.* I saw no evidence that any one of these men wanted to institute social, economic or religious reforms. Most were irritated because they did not have a greater say in government, because Qaddhafi was a 'despot' and because they wanted 'power'. They used this word constantly. I also attended clandestine meetings of middle-aged, middle-class civilians of the old regime—that

* One was killed in a road accident while I was there and within hours men were whispering to one another, 'One down, eleven to go.'

of King Idris—who were more concerned about gaining for Libya a better image in the world, giving Libyans better living conditions, and getting rid of the Egyptians who had been imported to show the backward Libyans how to run their country. The contrast between the aspirations of these older men and the young officers was startling.

No one seriously suggests the mechanical transference of political systems from distant countries to the Arab states. If the Arab peoples, as Arab monarchists and militarists argue, have not yet matured for a democratic life, they should be educated for it. But there is no worse educational system than beatings and arbitrary orders. Officer-politicians regard their people with contempt and suspicion; they see independent forces as factors leading to destruction and anarchy and crush them. The Arab nation does contain great creative forces which would transform society if only allowed to grow. Before about 1945 many excellent writers, thinkers, political leaders and communal workers were active in the Arab lands. But from the moment the officer-politicians seized power, they never encouraged them; creative forces are stifled. For example, the writers of the best works in modern Egyptian literature published their important books before 1952. The crop since then has been poor.

After seizing power through coups, officer-politicians usually promise that 'when the time comes' they will return to their barracks and hand the government over to elected representatives of the people. They never do; military rule does not get rid of itself, it merely changes its leaders. It is axiomatic that no kind of dictatorship—revolutionary, proletarian, monarchic, military or fascist—is self-liquidating.

With Army and occasionally Air Force officers so obviously in command of the civil structure, it is not surprising that the Arab populace has come to accept as normal a situation that could hardly be envisaged in the West. Military rule has inhibited thought and expression and instances of outspoken comment—such as that of the young Syrian lieutenant mentioned earlier—become all the more startling. The threat of force is omnipresent so that liberal, creative thinkers tend to keep their thoughts to themselves—except in Lebanon. This is inevitable when officer-politicians act like commanders who regard the civil population as if they were military subordinates in some bold operation, owing obedience on pain of being considered mutineers or enemies.

For as long as Service officers control the government of the Arab countries, the whole administrative system and the nation's media, the Arab mind—including that of officers—cannot develop its imaginative and lively potential.

Cecil Hourani expresses the feelings of most Arab thinkers: 'The military regimes which have installed themselves in Arab countries since 1949 had their only justification in terms of the necessity of meeting external dangers. They have given a demonstration of their incompetence in war. What reason do we have to suppose that they are likely to be more successful in economic planning and development, in education, foreign affairs, finance or culture?'*

* In *Al-Nahar*, Beirut, November 1967.

10 *Attitudes to Israel and the West*

'The extermination of Israel is a prerequisite for the preservation of Arabism and the renaissance of the Arabs.' *The Arab Homeland and Its Foreign Relations*, a Syrian high school textbook, the Co-operative Printing House, Damascus, 1964.

'The Arabs are the innocent victims with which the West has atoned for its sins against the Jews.' Naji Alush, *The Journey to Palestine*, Beirut, 1964.

'I am glad Israel exists; through her we can bring about the real Arab revolution.' Ghassan Kanafani, spokesman for the Popular Front for the Liberation of Palestine, to the author, Beirut, January 1972. Kanafani was referring to the social revolution; the Arabs, he believed, could only be united through common enmity to a foreign 'enemy'. Soon after, he was murdered by a bomb placed in his car.

Since 1948 it has been impossible to study the Arab world without reference to Israel. To write a book about the Arab mind and omit any mention of the influence of Israel on that mind would be like writing a history of Britain and omitting the monarchy. The picture would be as incomplete. Arab thought is influenced by individual, group and national attitudes to Israel, especially in Lebanon, Syria, Iraq, Jordan, Egypt, and Kuwait. Saudi Arabia, though a near neighbour of Israel, has not been so concerned, other than through the efforts of Egypt to involve the Saudis in the dispute. Israel is probably the most frequent topic of conversation in all these Arab countries and among urban Algerians. I cannot recall ever having sat with a group of Arabs without the topic quickly arising. Clearly, then, the contemporary Arab mind cannot be understood without an analysis of attitudes to Israel.

An outsider can only deplore the desperately unhappy situation, the more so when he knows that Judaism and Islam are sister religions with some important resemblances. Hebrew and Arabic are cognate languages; a Hebraist could learn Arabic and a Talmudist could understand the holy law of Islam with greater sympathy and ease than a Christian scholar. Jewish scholars were among the first to present Islam—as the Moslems themselves see it—to European readers. These same Jews stressed and romanticized the merits and achievements of Moslem civilization in its great days, when it was a constructively inspiring force. The Jews, from centuries before the concept of Israel, subscribed to Islam's 'five rights of man'—to preserve his religion, to preserve his life, to preserve his children, to preserve his possessions and to preserve his reason. The traditional relationship between Moslems and Jews is strong, for both are descended from Shem (Genesis 10) and therefore Semitic.

The Jews of Asia Minor and later those of Israel have never been 'against' the Arabs. In speaking to hundreds of Israeli soldiers I met only two—they were Yemeni Jews—who 'hated' the Arabs; but I have met only a few Arab soldiers who do not hate the Israelis, a hatred almost wholly manufactured through indoctrination.

Long before Israel existed, hatred—and probably fear—manifested itself in violence. Led by Haj Amin al-Husseini, later appointed Mufti of Jerusalem, President of the Supreme Moslem Council and Chairman of the Arab Higher Committee, Arab mobs in April 1920 attacked Jews in Jerusalem, killing 5 and wounding more than 200. The following year 47 Jews were killed and 146 wounded by Arab terrorist attacks. In 1929, 133 Jews were massacred and 339 wounded in the ancient Jewish religious centres of Hebron and Safad. The Jewish community in Hebron was forced to abandon the city until 1967.

Between 1936 and 1939 Arab terrorists attacked isolated Jewish villages, buses and cars; 517 Jews were killed. Jews were not the only victims of terrorism. On October 15, 1938, the Jerusalem correspondent of the *New York Times* reported: 'Extremist Arab followers of the Mufti . . . are rapidly achieving their aims by eliminating political opponents in Palestine who are inclined toward moderation. More than 90 per cent of the total casualties in the past few days have been inflicted by Arab terrorists on Arabs.'

In the year before Israel was declared a state, Azam Pasha, Secretary of the Arab League, was threatening 'a war of extermination and a momentous massacre [of the British, the Jews and collaborating Arabs] which will be spoken of like the Mongolian massacre of the Crusades'.

A common mistake in the West is to look on the Middle East situation as 'the Arabs versus the Israelis'. This is naïve and ill-informed for Arabs themselves see it quite differently. To them Israel is a bastion of imperialism, and the Israelis are representatives of the hostile Western world. Israel was planted at the heart of the Arab world for various vicious purposes which Nasser himself explained.* 'Our Arab countries have not ceased for centuries to be the goal of the imperialists' attacks and enmity, as if imperialism wanted to avenge an ancient wrong on the nation that brought civilization to their countries with the conquests of the Caliphate after Mohammad.'

Nasser explains that imperialism has assumed many guises. When the Crusades were exposed another open campaign started, without any attempt to conceal European aims. This was open imperialism, which tried to impose its rule in order

'. . . to degrade us and acquire what was in our hands and under our feet, to exploit our wealth and our markets for its own benefit, to take our lands as a base for its armies, so that they should consume the fruits of our land in peace and destroy our buildings with their own hands or by the hands of their enemies in war, after which they would sow the seeds

* In an introduction entitled 'Imperialism', bearing Nasser's autograph signature, to a book published in April 1954 as No. 2 in the 'Chosen For You' series and called *Leaders of the Imperialist Gangs*.

of corruption and dissension among us, liquidate the foundations of our nationality and muzzle us to prevent our recalling the grandeur of our past, deaden our hearts to make us insensible of our glorious achievements, and steal away our minds and this world of ours.'

Speaking of the Crusades, Nasser said on his return from a tour of Syria, March 20, 1958, 'It was England and France that attacked this region under the name of the Crusades, and the Crusades were nothing else but British-French imperialism . . . it was no accident at all that General Allenby, commander of the British forces, said on arriving in Jerusalem [1917]: "Today the wars of the Crusaders are completed." Nor is it in any way an accident that when General Gouraud [Free French commander] arrived in Damascus, he visited the tomb of Saladin and said "Behold we have returned, Saladin." ' (Saladin was *not* an Arab but a Persian.)

Long before Nasser made his speech the Arabs had perverted religious belief into religious prejudice and the deliberate cultivation of intolerance. The expeditions of Mohammad against the Jews of the Arabian peninsula had left their mark, as every action of the Prophet was accepted as a model of conduct. This history is exploited in modern times for purely political ends, as in *Al-Ahram* (26.11.55): 'Our war against the Jews is an old struggle that began with Mohammad and in which he achieved many great victories. . . . It is our duty to fight the Jews for the sake of Allah and religion, and it is our duty to end the war that Mohammad began.'

The Arabs have since drawn virtually the entire world into 'the Middle East conflict' so again it is important that we understand Arab thinking about Israel. Generalizations are safe because attitudes differ only in degree; for instance, hatred in Syria is reduced to hostility in Tunisia. Westernized Arabs are not typical of the hundred million others; those who have lived for any time in the West merely pay lip service to the idea of annihilating Israel.

And annihilation or liquidation is the principal attitude. It is presented as a task of universal importance because it will rectify an 'injustice' of fundamental historical significance, 'the greatest crime in the annals of mankind'—the establishment of the State of Israel. Thus Chapter 10 of the Egyptian National Charter states: 'The insistence of our people on liquidating the Israeli aggression on a part of the Palestine land is a determination to liquidate one of the most dangerous pockets of imperialist resistance against the struggle of peoples. . . . Our pursuit [*sic*] of the Israeli policy of infiltration in Africa is only an attempt to limit the spread of a destructive imperialist cancer.'

In their struggle against Israel the Arabs believe they are playing a part in the global war between the forces of liberation and the forces of oppression, between good and evil. The liquidation will also be an event of historic importance because 'The solution of the Palestine problem will pave the way to the solution of world problems.'*

Sadat made the Arab position clear when speaking to the Egyptian National Council on June 2, 1971: 'The Zionist conquest to which we are being subjected will not be terminated by the return of the occupied territories. This is a new Crusaders' war which will persist during our generation and through the coming one. It is our duty . . . to arm and fortify the new generation and equip it with the strength to be able to continue the struggle after we are gone.'

Because they talk so much about Arab unity and because it eludes them the Arabs focus blame on that alien group which is nearest to hand—the Israelis. They seem to forget that the Arab world was divided for long periods, while they remember and emphasize the brief periods of unity, which are presented as typical of their entire history. Rejection and selectivity are accompanied by an active process of relegation of inconvenient facts to the subconscious, which becomes a reservoir of information and images that a person wishes to ignore. A double

* The journal *Filastin*, July 26, 1952.

system of images—in the conscious and in the sub-conscious—is created. But the repressed images still exist in a twilight zone, and sometimes emerge and become conscious. This process, 'the return of the repressed' in Freud's term, leads to ambivalence in regard to the enemy—there is a dual image of him: good and evil. For example, the Arabs tend to regard Israel in negative terms, but sometimes they present her as an example to themselves—military prowess is an instance—the good qualities which have been repressed thus rising to the surface.

Perhaps what distresses the Arab most of all is their loss of 'greatness'. Professor Cantwell Smith, formerly director of the Institute of Islamic Studies at McGill University, Canada, later Professor of Comparative Religion at Harvard, explains that this sense is particularly strong among Arabs. The aspiration or the claim to greatness is not peculiar to Arabs but among them it is connected with religion and history. Other faiths, like Christianity, won their hold slowly, and their beginnings are associated with persecution, but Islam achieved greatness immediately. A few years after Mohammad, the Arabs burst out of the Arabian Peninsula and established an even larger empire than that of the Romans. This they regarded as the work of Allah who granted them victory to demonstrate the truth of their religion. Since then, Smith points out, historical, secular success was regarded as an integral part of Islam; success and Islam were inseparable. The Arabs are more sensitive to this feeling than other Moslems who adopted Islam as a result of its success.

When Europe showed its superiority and—even more—when the Middle East came under the rule of Christian peoples, the Arabs suffered a profound shock. Smith finds proof of this in the flood of apologetic works which try to explain how it is impossible that they are neither successful nor 'great'.

This flood of books continues and some of its themes are constantly repeated in Arab writings, speeches and newspaper articles. The aim is to explain that it is not the Arabs who are to blame for their backwardness, but malevolent foreign factors.

169

It is the enemy's intrigues, motivated by fear of Arab competition, that have made them backward. In itself the assertion that the big Western Powers are the enemy tends to enhance the Arab's self-respect.

The apologetic religious and spiritual trend merges with the secularist national trend. The claim to greatness makes the feeling of inferiority and frustration doubly painful. Hostility to the West is the product of the feeling that the Arabs have been robbed of their 'greatness'. One can understand their bitterness and humiliation at being 'robbed of a country' —which is also evidence of their failure and redoubles the agony and the indignation. The belief in their own greatness limits the capacity of the Arabs to find any fault in themselves.

Another explanation is that Arab society is marked by its atomization; there is little internal unity and co-operation, and every individual is hostile to his neighbour. Constant internal bickering at any level is externalized by the frequent ascription of blame to others and a deep consciousness of hostility.

The Israelis are the obvious target for this hostility. The virulence of propaganda against them is remarkable even in a century which has seen Nazi propaganda against the Jews, Russian propaganda against the United States, American propaganda against Germany (1915–18) and Hindu and Moslem propaganda against each other.

The Arabs have enlisted Mohammad for defamatory purpose, with such statements as, 'The Jews of our time are the descendants of the Jews who harmed the Prophet'; or, 'The Prophet enlightened us about the right way to treat the Jews. . . . We must follow this way and purify holy Palestine from their filth. . . .' The Jewish God suffers in comparison with the Arab God. He is 'bloodthirsty, fickle-minded, harsh and greedy. He is pleased with imposture and deceit.'

Hate is engendered and nurtured in children, so that a twelve-year-old child in Egypt, doing an exercise in Arabic grammar, encounters the sentence: 'The Arabs do not cease to act for the extermination of Israel.' Concluding a lesson in history a Jordanian book says, 'So you boys and girls must cling to the slogan "Israel must be destroyed"'.

Understandably, the Palestinians, who believe the Israelis dispossessed them, are outstandingly prone to the use of defamatory terms about Israel and the Jews, but they are by no means alone. Nashashibi describes the Jews whom he saw from the walls while on a visit to Jerusalem as: '. . . a collection of the world's hooligans and its garbage. . . . Dogs, robbers, clear out to your own countries!' In another passage he describes Israel as '. . . an international dung-heap in which the squalor of the whole world has been collected.'

In an academic publication, the *Egyptian Political Science Review*, which is issued by the Egyptian Association for Political Science, we find: 'And thus Britain wanted to exhaust the strength of the Arabs and divide them, and at one and the same time to get rid of the Zionist plague in her country. She assembled these thousands of vagabonds and aliens, bloodsuckers and pimps and said to them, "Take for yourselves a national home called Israel." Thus the dregs of the nations were collected in the Holy Land.'*

One of the strangest and strongest ideas among Arabs is that Israel was created as a creature of British imperialism. In fact, it was established in defiance of the British. It emerged as a result of a prolonged campaign of civil disobedience and armed struggle by Jews against the British administration of Palestine. When the British, after failing to defeat a prolonged Jewish insurgency, vacated the country, they hoped that the Arabs would accomplish what they themselves had failed to achieve. There is even ground for belief that the British hoped to return to Palestine behind the victorious Arab Legion, which they directly commanded, equipped and financed.

Abusive language has a cathartic function; it substitutes a verbal assault for a real one and abuse becomes a consolation

* Fathi 'Uthman al-Mahlawi, 'A Spearhead Against Arab Nationalism', in a special issue of the *Journal of Arab Nationalism*, January–March 1959.

for impotence and a means of relief. It appears that catharsis is a frequent feature of the Arabic use of words. The terms of abuse may also have a further, symbolic function. By showering disgrace on the object they make him even more loathsome and abhorrent.

Abuse conveys an instruction to the abuser. If something is described as filth, pollution and excrement, then the need for cleansing and sanitary action is implicit. If the enemy is described as a cancer or a malignant growth, the implication is that a surgical operation is needed to excise it. Such expressions are probably manifestations of the political and genocidal claim. Since Mohammad, Islam has regarded the Jews, basically, as subordinate and inferior, in fulfilment of the Koran's decree that the Jews must be kept in a lowly position. The independent Jewish State established in 1948 was, therefore, a great offence. Mohammad fought and defeated the Jews, but now the wheel of history has come full turn and the Jews have defeated Moslems. Islam aspires to territorial expansion which makes the establishment of a Jewish State, trespassing on Islamic territory, an intolerable provocation.

All this goes back to the 1948 war which Arabs generally describe as 'the disaster' or 'the great defeat'. In this war, the Jews, who had been described as 'gangs' and regarded as doomed in misery and degradation, were revealed as a dangerous opponent. Derision gave place to hatred. For the Palestinian Arabs, the defeat was a confirmation of the Jew's power. For the others, it was the beginning of a direct knowledge of the Israelis.

For many it was a great disaster for all Arabs and Moslems. Israel is regarded as a wedge in the heart of the 'Arab region' at a spot of strategic importance, the gateway to the Middle East and a bridge between the continents. From an historical point of view, the defeat was described as a more grievous disaster than the loss of Spain in 1492. It was a material, spiritual and moral blow, a racial degradation. The decline of the Arabs and their subjection to foreign rule reached a climax

172

with their defeat by the Jews. An emotional and ideological shock, it deprived the rulers of their peoples' respect, and undermined their legitimacy. It opened up an era of revolutions, shook the Arabs' faith in their heroic self-image and led to an inter-Arab crisis of confidence.

King Hussein said, in explaining the results of the defeat, 'Many of us lost our self-confidence and our trust in our capacity to act and restore the rights. We began to be suspicious of one another. The Arab States began to accuse each other to evade responsibility.'*

President Nasser spoke of 'entering Palestine on a carpet of blood'; on another occasion, May 31, 1965, 'The road to the liberation of Palestine is strewn not with roses but with blood. It will be restored by force when we decide.' In May 1966 Hafez Assad, then the Syrian Minister for Defence, was equally violent: 'We shall never call for, or accept peace. We shall only accept war and the restoration of our usurped land. We have resolved to drench this land with our blood, to oust you aggressors and throw you into the sea for good.' King Hussein urged his people 'to kill the Jews wherever you find them, kill them with your hands, with your nails and teeth'.

After such violent language expressing such supreme confidence, another military defeat in six days—the June 1967 war—intensified the Arabs' hatred to such an extent that they were consumed by thoughts of revenge. Mohammad Haikal expressed it succinctly in an editorial in *Al-Ahram* on February 25, 1971: 'There are only two well-defined goals on the Arab scene: erasing the traces of the 1967 aggression by Israel's withdrawal from all the areas occupied by it in that year and erasing the aggression of 1948 by Israel's total and absolute annihilation. This is not really a well-defined goal, but an oversimplified one; and the mistake of some of us is starting off with the last step before beginning the first.'

By this time the fiercest verbal violence was emanating from the fedayeen (terrorist) groups, such as Fatah.

* Amman Radio, May 22, 1963, 14.00 hours.

'The liberation action is not only the removal of an armed imperialist base; but, more important—it is the destruction of a society. Our armed violence will be expressed in many ways. In addition to the destruction of the military force of the Zionist occupying state, it will also be turned towards the destruction of the means of life of Zionist society in all their forms—industrial, agricultural and financial. The armed violence must seek to destroy the military, political, economic, financial and ideological institutions of the Zionist occupying state, so as to prevent all possibility of the growth of a new Zionist society. The aim of the Palestine Liberation War is not only to inflict a military defeat but also to destroy the Zionist character of the occupied land, whether it is human or social.'*

The main weapon in the propaganda campaign is the radio because Arabs are conditioned and responsive to the spoken word much more than the written. T. E. Lawrence noted how the Arabs could be swept away by an idea or a feeling, 'or swung as if on a cord', especially if the idea be expressed in sonorous, imprecise and hyperbolic language. Constant radio agitation and provocation, playing on this built-in susceptibility has them permanently off-balance, excited by resounding words.

Propaganda is a dangerous tool, to be used for short periods only or it backfires. Some of the results of Arab propaganda have been pathetic. An American ship loaded with wheat tried to unload its cargo in Beirut after having stopped in Haifa. The ship was forced to go to Cyprus to 'cleanse itself' and then it was allowed to unload in Beirut.

A foreigner travelling in the Middle East and wishing to move from an Arab country to Israel can do so only via Cyprus. To make a booking in, say, Beirut, one goes to the Cyprus Air offices and asks for a ticket to 'the other place'. This

* *The Liberation of the Occupied Lands and the Struggle Against Direct Imperialism*, pamphlet No. 8 in a Fatah series, *Revolutionary Studies and Experiments*.

is Tel Aviv, but the name cannot be mentioned. On the printed Cyprus Air flights-schedule no reference is made to the existence of a service between Nicosia and Tel Aviv because this would incense the Arabs, who will tolerate it only if it is not publicized.

Films with Jewish actors, or actors who are known for their sympathies for Israel, may be boycotted. Films with Elizabeth Taylor often could not be shown because she was married either to Mike Todd or Eddie Fisher, both Jewish. Sal Mineo, who played a major role in *Exodus*, Frank Sinatra, and Danny Kaye have been taboo at one time or another. The Disney film, *The Sleeping Beauty*, could not be shown in Lebanon because the horse was called Samson, a well-known name in the Old Testament. The censor wanted to change the name to Simson, but since this would have required a new soundtrack *Sleeping Beauty* was never shown. Charles Malik, a respected Arab politician, was highly criticized because he visited the Israeli pavilion of the Brussels International Fair.

Omar Sharif was discredited because he kissed Barbra Streisand, a Jewish actress, in *Funny Girl*. He regained his popularity when the word was spread that a stand-in had been used in the offensive scenes. Syrian, Jordanian and Lebanese Arabs will not co-operate with Israelis on irrigation plans, though these would benefit them immediately.

Atlases used in Arab schools do not show Israel. In the teachers' training college near Ein el-Hilwe, South Lebanon, I asked an instructor what would happen if a student teacher drew a map and included Israel. 'She would be punished for telling an untruth,' he said. 'There is no such place as Israel.' Yet threats against Israel and the Jews are included in almost every lesson of the day and in ritualistic school assemblies.

Tragically, the obsession about Israel is limiting the Arabs' vision and taking up too much of their intellectual and emotional energy. Many scholars spend virtually all their working time on anti-Jewish diatribes, some of which are bizarre and crude. Dr Abdullah al-Tall, in a lengthy book, *The Danger of World Jewry to Islam*, explains in his introduction: 'The God

175

of the Jews is not satisfied with animal sacrifices; he must be appeased with human sacrifices. Hence the Jewish custom of slaughtering children and extracting their blood to mix it with their matzot on Passover.'*

According to al-Tall, the child is placed in a barrel equipped with numerous hollow needles which pierce his body and through which the blood flows into drainage pipes. This kind of killing is extremely painful, to the satisfaction of the Jews, who believe that the suffering purifies the blood they collect. The Jews also kill adults, al-Tall says, and are particularly pleased if the victim is one of their friends and an innocent man, for they believe that by killing they are fulfilling a sacred religious duty which will win them a special blessing.

It would be some consolation to report that Dr al-Tall's appalling lies are a rare and extreme case; but they are merely typical. Thousands of books in Arabic are filled with such stories. Nearly all of them develop their themes to the conclusion that the redemption of the world will come with the disappearance of the Jews. This is why Dr al-Tall can call Adolph Eichmann 'a martyr who fell in the holy war'.

Mohammad Darwaza, an Egyptian, went to some trouble to catalogue the evil characteristics which he says are ascribed to the Jews by the Koran:

'Unbelief, denial, quarrelsome, provocative behaviour, selfishness, hardheartedness, arrogance, boastfulness, self-aggrandizement and assumption of superiority, lack of sincere devotion and stable loyalty to anything, deception, machination, fraud, intrigue, lust for the possessions of others, deep envy even when they enjoy greater comfort, efforts to dominate everything, efforts to influence everyone, contempt for all restrictions, assumption of the right to take over the property of others, denial of responsibility towards others, miserliness, vice and immorality, lack of reciprocity

* Published by Dar al-Qalam, affiliated with the National Publishing Institute, Cairo, 1964.

in friendship and in assurance of loyalty, involvement in every base and immoral situation, cowardice. . . .'*

By attributing all these shortcomings to the Koran—where many are not even indirectly mentioned—Darwaza automatically makes them incontestable to his fellow Arab Moslems.

The ultimate effect of the constant flow of anti-Jewish broadcasts and writings has the inevitable effect of making the great mass of Arabs callous and barbarous. Hence, when three terrorists crossed into Israel from Lebanon in April 1974 and murdered eighteen townspeople of Qiryat Shemona the deed was publicly applauded throughout the Arab world. Yet the victims included five women and eight children. One of the terrorists was aged 28, the others 20; they had a lifelong indoctrination of hatred so to them the killing of any Israeli was not only justifiable but righteous. For the same reason Arab leaders can be 'proud' of the terrorist murderers, who knew they were setting out on a suicide mission, but like the Assassins of old were sure that they would arrive in the gardens of delight as promised by the Koran. In any case, as I have already mentioned, in Arab thought the victim is responsible for his own suffering.

An even bloodier massacre was that at Maalot, May 15, 1974, when three terrorists, who were aged 27, 22 and 19, took over a school and killed twenty Israelis and wounded seventy, nearly all children. These two events marked the beginning of a campaign against Israel's children. At the time President Sadat was urging Syria to agree to Henry Kissinger's plan for disengagement on the Golan Heights while, simultaneously, Cairo Radio was urging the terrorists to 'kill and destroy'.

Arab leaders professed themselves 'proud' of the terrorist murderers of Qiryat Shemona and Maalot, a logical enough pride considering the decades of vituperation against the Israelis to which the Arabs had subjected themselves. The

* *The History of the Children of Israel from their Books*, Cairo, 1960.

terrorists who caused so much havoc knew they had little chance of surviving their exploits. And it is worth saying again that in Arab thought the victim is responsible for his own suffering. Against all this it is pointless to appeal to conscience and ask, 'How can you wage war on children?' Given a life-time's indoctrination a man can wage war on anyone.

Many Westerners and Israelis think that since Israel has more than once demonstrated that it is stronger than the Arabs, the only rational thing for Arabs to do is to stop terrorism and war and make peace. But the situation is not governed by this kind of logic, for objectivity is not a value in the Arab system. 'For the Arabs, defeat does not generate a desire for peace; instead, it produces an emotional need for revenge, and this need is deepened rather than attenuated by each successive defeat.'*

In the case of Egypt, the part-victory of the October 1973 War—recovering the Suez Canal—might reduce the need for further revenge, but this will never apply to Syria and Iraq, nor to the Palestinians.

Israel is a convenient excuse for almost every internal ill in every Arab country, and even for personal troubles. A travel agent in Benghazi, Libya, told me that Israel is to blame for the lack of prosperity in the travel business. In fact, the Libyan Government discourages tourism. Such rationalizing comes easily to the Arab mind. In September 1969 the fourth con-ference of the Academy of Islamic Research took place in Cairo. No fewer than eighteen papers were presented to the conference and every one contains many references to the Jews and Israel. One paper, entitled 'Jewish role in aggression on the Islamic base in Medina', concerns history which is thirteen centuries old. Three talks concerned the jihad. Another, by Kamal Ahmad Own, vice-principal of an Islamic institute, was entitled 'The Jews are the enemies of human life as is evident from their holy book'.

Such is the pre-occupation with Israel. Such is the problem the West must face.

* Harold W Glidden, *American Journal of Psychiatry*, February 1972.

Still, it is some encouragement to know that at least half a million Arabs—the so-called Israeli Arabs—live in amity with the Israelis. These are the people and their children who stayed in Palestine when Israel was declared a state; they do not include the Arabs of the 'occupied' territories. The Israeli Arabs include about 350,000 Moslems and 77,000 Christians, and these groups appear to live on relaxed terms with each other as well as with the Israelis. The benefits of economic co-operation are so evident that the Israeli Arabs, who are full Israeli citizens, have settled into a placid live-and-let-live existence with the Israelis.

But the Arab mind, even in these circumstances, is so inflexible that total integration is many years away. This is sometimes shown in startling ways. In the Department of Arabic Studies at the University of Jerusalem in 1973 the professor had roughly equal numbers of Israeli and Israeli Arab students and he asked each group to put itself in the place of the other and argue a case for their right to the territory which constitues the State of Israel. In other words, in Arabic language, the Israelis were to argue the Arab case and the Arabs the Israeli case. Ample time for preparation was given and the professor believed that his Arab students, being more eloquent, would present a better case than the Israelis. The Israeli and Arab students selected to speak were to talk alternately and the Israelis, one by one, duly stated their arguments for the Arab 'cause'. The Arabs, however, were unable to speak. They simply could not put themselves in somebody else's shoes. It was not a matter of their resenting the exercise or of collusion to embarrass the professor and their Israeli fellow-students. Psychologically, they could not even come to terms with the extraordinary situation of having to think themselves into a new role. The incident is significant for foreign students of the Middle East scene.

11 *The Inner Conflict*

'Where to—if Allah wills?' Arab taxi-driver's usual greeting to his fare.

'It was the Arab leaders who were responsible for starting the June War. They had duped themselves with their own fiery rhetoric and had become prisoners of their own propaganda.' Evan M. Wilson, a former U.S. Minister-Consul General who served in Beirut, Cairo, Teheran and Jerusalem, in *Jerusalem, Key to Peace*, 1970.

The Arabs need their social, cultural, agricultural and educational revolutions. They do *not* need continual armed revolutions. Least of all can they afford to indulge in wars, though it should be stated that the concept of holy war is not unique to Islam. Judaism and Christianity preceded it in sanctifying bloodshed in God's name, and in intolerance towards unbelievers they usually surpassed it.

The important point is that only in Islam has the religious sanction of political power continued into the late twentieth century. To separate church and state as a principle has little appeal in Islam, as Ali 'Abd al-Raziq found in 1925 when he was bold enough to advocate* such separation. Though he held the rank of Sheikh, al-Raziq was expelled from al-Azhar, the Cairo religious university, and disqualified from holding any religious office.

In 1903 one of the most perceptive of Egyptian writers, Farah Autun, had warned the Arab world that states controlled by religion are weak. Religious authorities are weak by nature, he said, since they are at the mercy of the feelings of the mass and in society they emphasize what *divides* men. To mix religion

* In his book, *Islam and the Principles of Government*, Cairo, 1925.

with politics weakens religion itself because it is brought down into the gore of the arena. Religious interference in government inevitably leads to war, Autun said most seriously of all, if only because the different religious sects will always be hostile to one another, and since religious loyalties are strong among the masses it is always possible to stir up their feelings. Unfortunately, Arab governments used Autun's work not as a warning but as encouragement. They did that which he told them not to do—they used religion for political ends.

The position is desperate but not without solution. The Arab world needs statesmen who can, for the sake of their own peoples, put an end to the obsession about Israel, and who will not use Israel as a way of diverting attention from acute internal problems. Even more, the Arabs need a Mustapha Kemal (Kemal Ataturk), whose greatest achievement was to separate State and Religion. Through his foresight and drive, the lot of the Turkish people vastly improved in two generations. And they found that they did not need to renounce Islam to achieve this.

Islam today is not the normative framework for the group and the individual that it was a century ago. New beliefs weakened the religious faith of many to the point of indifference and heresy, and created fresh ties of identification and loyalty. Yet Islam has remained a mighty public and emotional force; links with the community of Islam have remained strong even for most of those who have abandoned it as a faith. In the Arab world it has merged with nationalism, influenced it, and been influenced by it. This Arab nationalist mentality with an Islamic colouring is more self-confident and aggressive in the independent countries than when it was under foreign domination, and more so in the 1970s than in the 1920s. The liberal period in Arab thinking and politics of the 1920s has ended. Nationalism, nourished by Islamic tradition and thinking, is at the top of the scale of values. The purely religious aspect of Islam has become weakened, but the communal and political aspects have gained new momentum.

The writing of the Middle East is changing. Rational, logical, and consistent thought and expression are a matter of intellectual training as much as the result of environmental influences. A transitional society in conflict with its traditional forms of organization can produce only a fragmented, organically unrelated thought process. Many of the forms of contemporary ideology in the Middle East do not stem from the direct social experience of society, but are borrowed from abroad. Arab intellectuals agonize over the application to their own society of ideas and concepts developed in the West through centuries of consistent intellectual development. These intellectuals refer continually to a crisis of thought and spirit caused by the struggle between the past and the future, between materialism and spiritualism. The crisis will be resolved, many feel, through the discovery of an ideology that will galvanize all the dormant virtues of the Arab soul.

'The Arab world has a much greater inner conflict than any it insists on fighting with outsiders,' one of Libya's few well-educated women has told me. 'It is a conflict between a developed minority and a regressive majority. The outcome is rebirth or destruction.' She believes that a rebirth is possible but the feeling of some genuine Arab intellectuals who have moved to the West and can thus see their nation in perspective is gloomy. Professor Abdul Said of the American University, Washington D.C., says that 'Arab streets are filled with the debris of frustrated dreams and abandoned schemes as each new prophet attacks his predecessor with gay abandon. . . . Imprisoned in seemingly hopeless economic and social conditions, the Arab's response is similar to the howling of a caged wolf, for it is less a demonstration of virility than a function of self preservation and a release of frustration.'

Perhaps King Abdullah of Jordan was illustrating this function and release in a speech of September 1947 when opening the Islamic Cultural College in Amman. 'I hope and pray that our religious and intellectual institutions will continue to preach . . . and to create a new, vigorous Arab generation which is possessed of all virtues and ideals *that give it mastery over the earth* [my italics]. . . .'

This idea of mastery is the Arabs' own stumbling block. Yet some Arab minds are vital and courageous enough to speak their sincerity. Kamal Muruwa, the Beirut publisher who greatly admired Turkey, which he regarded as a truly Moslem country, believed that Turkish reforms, rather than destroying Islam, actually strengthened it by separating its spiritual aspects from politics. In September 1963 he wrote in his newspaper, *Al-Hayat*, a piece he entitled 'O Arabs of Sound Minds Unite!' The principal paragraph is:

'In several Arab countries, the young have taken over power. They maintain themselves from one country to another by using intimidation and bluff. They make war, giving the impression of being millions, although they are only a handful. Come! Stir yourselves from Morocco to Kuwait so that reason, probity and honesty may reign among Arabs instead of unrest, betrayal and stagnation.'

Nasser's agents assassinated Muruwa but a growing number of other Arabs are prepared to speak their minds because of —and not despite—his murder. The example which follows seems an apt one with which to conclude this book: 'For too long the field of publicity and expression has been left in the hands of professional demagogues, blackmailers and semi-educated fanatics. Our silence on the one hand, their vociferation on the other, have led the Arab world not merely to disaster but to the brink of disintegration. This is due primarily to *a psychological weakness in us: that* [which] *we do not like we pretend does not exist.*'*

---

* Cecil Hourani, for ten years adviser to President Bourguiba of Tunisia, in 'The Moment of Truth', an essay published in *El Nahar*, Beirut, which appeared in English in *Encounter*, November 1967. Hourani's italics.

Index

Arabic words and names are not indexed under the definite article 'Al' or 'El' but under the word or name following this.

185

Index

Blunt, Wilfred, 99
Bourguiba, Habib, 156n 183*n*
Bukhari, al-, 48
Burton, Richard, 59

caliphs, 21, 46–47
childrearing, 100–1, 145–46
children, 79, 126–27, 135, 170–71
chivalry, 64, 99
Christianity, 16, 29, 31–32, 39, 139, 179, 180; compared with Islam, 48, 59, 60, 169
Church and State relationship, 31, 41, 43, 48–49, 53, 57, 156, 180–81
Cohen, Elie, 115
commerce, 16, 48*n*, 139
communication. *See* gestures; language
Communist Party, 112, 118
conformity, 83–84, 90–91, 145–46
Copts, 60, 126
coups d'état, 23, 109–11, 125–26, 162; Egyptian, 127, 154–55; Iraqi, 115–16, 117, 127, 159; Jordanian, 128; Libyan, 161; vs. revolution, 161–62; Syrian, 86, 111, 127, 152–53, 160. *See also* assassinations; violence
criticism, Arab obsession with, 24, 25–26, 141. *See also* blame; self-criticism
Cromer, Evelyn Baring, Lord, 31
Crusades, 50, 51, 58, 166–67, 168
culture, 19, 67–68, 140, 146, 162
Cyprus, 174–75

Daghestani, Kazem, 89, 101
Darwaza, Mohammad, 176–77
Dawood, N.J., 34–35
diet, Koran on, 35
divorce, 90, 102
Druze sect, 114
Duke, Charles, 133

education: of Army officers, 153–54; Khaldun on, 56–57; and language, 68, 72–76, 179; and propaganda, 170–71, 175
Egypt, 22*n*, 60, 86, 93, 111, 115*n*, 139, 156; Army officers of, 156–57; coups in, 127, 154–55; and Israel, 164, 168; "Liberation Province," 158; terrorism in, 126, 130; violence in, 121–27
Eichmann, Adolf, 176
evil eye, 96, 145

"Fahlawi personality," 143
failure, fear of, 23, 93–94, 141–42, 143
Faisal, King of Saudi Arabia, 131
Faisal II, King of Iraq, 117
family: dependence on, 149; honor of, 92–93, 101, 103; violence in, 126–27
Farouk I, King of Egypt, 80, 155
Fatah, 173–74
Fedden, Robin, 135
fellaheen, 139–40
Fisher, Benjamin, 126*n*
Fisher, Eddie, 175
France, 18, 111, 122, 167
"Free Officers," 156–57
friendship, 23; Koran on, 39, 40

Gairdner, W.H.T., 42*n*
generosity, 65–66, 96–97, 108, 148–49
Genghis Khan, 58
Genuine, The (Bukhari), 48
gestures, 79–80, 96
Ghazali, al-, 91
"ghouls," 145–46
Gibb, H.A.R., 27, 68
Gillespie, James, 96
Glubb, John, 133
Gouraud, Henri, 167
government: Khaldun on, 55–56; as religious community, 31, 41, 43, 48–49, 53, 57, 156, 180–81
Great Britain, 118, 122, 128, 133, 134–35, 155, 167, 171

Haddad, George, 152
hadith, 47
Hafez, Amin al-, 115, 153
Hafsa, 35
Haikal, Mohammad, 144, 160, 173
Hamady, Sania: on Arab psychology, 22, 23, 102, 144, 149; on shame, 83, 84, 90, 91, 93
Hamasa, 28
Hamid, Ahmed, 119–20
Hamid, Majid, 119–20
Hanna, George, 132
Haqqi, Yahya, 44
Haroun al-Rashid, Caliph, 118
Hasanayn, Majdi, 157–58
Hatim of Tayyi', 65–66
Hayat, Al- (newspaper), 110, 125, 141–42, 183
Hebron, 165

187

Index

Index

Syria (*continued*)
130, 145, 156; Army officers in, 157, 159–60; Assassins in, 50–52; coups in, 86, 111, 127, 152–53, 160; and Israel, 164, 167, 175, 177, 178; Jews in, 114–15; violence in, 110, 111–15

Ta'abbata Sharran, 64
Tall, Abdullah al-, 175–76
Taylor, Elizabeth, 175
Tel, Wasfi el-, 53, 129
terrorism: Assassin, 50–52; Palestinian, 20, 53, 106–7, 127, 129, 130, 165–66, 177–78. *See also* violence
Tha'alibi, al-, 15
theft, 39, 131
thought, Arab, 143, 182; and language, 68–71, 73–76
Todd, Mike, 175
torture, 107, 119–21; of prisoners-of-war, 113–15, 126. *See also* violence
Touqan, Fadwa, 76–77, 100
Toynbee, Arnold, 133–34
Transjordan, 128. *See also* Jordan
Tunisia, 22*n*, 58, 104, 107, 120, 156, 167
Turkey, 58, 109, 122, 156, 181, 183
Turki, Fawaz, 107

Ubayd Allal al-Khatib, 51
United Arab Emirates, 22*n*
United Arab Republic (UAR), 111, 115*n*, 155
'Uruba (Arabism), 140–41
Uthman, Caliph, 46

Vatikiosis, P.J., 108
vengeance. *See* revenge
violence, 23–24, 28, 61, 106–7, 109, 129–31; Egyptian, 121–27; in families, 126–27; Iraqi, 110, 111, 115–21, 159; against Jews, 165–66, 177–78; Jordanian, 127–29; Libyan, 130–31; in literature, 64, 77–78, 109; political, 23–24, 50–53, 108–9, 115, 117–18 (*see also* coups d'état); and prayer, 131; and shame, 84–85, 92; Syrian, 111–15
Von Grunebaum, G.E., 75, 142

Wahba, Hafiz, 46, 99–100
war. *See* jihad; names of specific wars
Westermarck, E.A., 23
Wilson, Evan, 180
women, 91, 157; Koran on, 35, 37, 38, 39, 59, 98, 99, 104–5; and literature, 66, 76–77, 78; and shame, 86–90, 92; status of, 64, 66, 98–105; as virgins, 35, 36–37, 86–89, 102, 103, 105

Yaguri, Assaf, 126
Yamani, Sheikh, 21
Yemen Arab Republic, 22*n*, 60, 111
Yom Kippur War. *See* October War

Za'im, Husni al-, 86, 111, 152, 156
Zaydan clan, 87–89
Zeidan, Abdullah, 89
Zeidan, Husniya, 89

190